Irish Banknotes
Irish Paper Money 1928 – 2001

By
Mártan Mac De

GU00691745

Printed in Ireland
by
Seachrán, P.O. Box 99, Kells, Co. Meath, Ireland.

Printed digitally in Dublin.
Cover design by Gosia Sitek.

When using this book as a source please quote it as a reference.

ISBN 9780954371234

British Library Cataloguing in Publication Data.
A catalogue record for this book is available from the British Library.

Preface

One of the most significant aspects of any collecting hobby is that of market valuations. During the past few years of economic depression and turmoil the value of many investment devices has collapsed. Although prices softened for many Irish banknotes they have recovered somewhat, and demand remained strong throughout for Irish small collectibles, including notes.

Around 2007 prices for Irish notes generally reached an all-time high for all types of material. Prices proceeded then to fall for various reasons and to a varying degree across the different series of banknotes, with common bank Ploughman £5 and £10 notes falling by up to 50% from their peak. The most severe fall was seen in Old pre-partition notes. Prices had become very bloated and collapsed by up to 80% in some cases. Chance favours the prepared mind as they say, and there were some nice bargains to be had for the canny collector around this time as a result.

However, rarer notes of the Lavery and Ploughman series, especially in high grade, held their value. These strengthened in price terms as they became sought-after by collectors looking for a worthwhile investment vehicle. This underlined the old adage that rarity with eye-appeal will always be desirable!

Places like ebay tend to set the price for lower grade notes. Fairly priced notes sell well. Overpriced notes do tend to not sell as collectors seek good value.

In the past few years there has been a good trickle of new material surfacing , particularly in Ploughman notes. This includes three previously unrecorded 1928 £100 notes to add to the census.

Most notably, for the first time ever in auction, a Nothern Bank Ploughman £10 note (illustrated) was offered by Whytes, Dublin in their History, Literature & Collectables auction of Sept 17, 2013. The note fetched €14,000 plus fees (approx €17,500), a very strong price. Although low grade (at "About fine" by Whytes) and somewhat fragile, the note still retains considerable eye appeal. Also, this note had not been recorded previously by the author, and it brings the count of verified (by serial number) Northern Bank £10 notes to 6. Nice to see the rarest Type note of all being tested in auction.

A survey of Ploughman and rarer Lavery notes has been underway for the past 15 years in an effort to determine the number of surviving notes potentially available to collectors, and relative rarities. A report on this will be published in the near future.

ACKNOWLEDGMENTS

Many collectors, too numerous to name here, contributed information to this book and its predecessors and some have loaned notes for illustration. Particular thanks go to the following for their kind and tireless assistance: W. Barrett, R. Cooke and T. Lenny. Special thanks also to officials of The Central Bank of Ireland who helped to arrange the granting of permission to reproduce illustrations for which the Central Bank of Ireland holds the copyright, and for the loan of specimens for illustration. Additionally, thanks is further expressed to the The National Museum of Ireland and The Bank of Ireland for providing access to information and for loaning some banknotes for illustration.

Thanks are expressed also to the following for major research assistance: G. MacAmhlaigh, L. G. Burr, J. Stafford-Langan, M. MacEvilly, N. Shirlaw, J. N. Simpson, R. Walshe, R. Woods. Acknowledgments for illustrated notes and for information received are not made individually for security reasons and because of the large number of persons who have supplied notes for illustration.

This book aims to be a basic catalogue of all Irish Government banknote issues and the Limerick Soviet notes of 1919. Valuations are conservitave estimates, based on auction results and sales.

Books of this kind are always a collective effort and are only possible with the assistance of the collecting community at large. This book is an assimilation of the knowledge and on-going research of many collectors, much of it started decades ago.

Copies of this book are available at the cover price plus postage and packing for as long as stocks last from: www.irishpapermoney.com or PO Box 99, Kells, Co. Meath, Ireland.

Litt A

The Structure of Irish Banknote Issues

The issues in the shaded areas are covered in this book

British Rule

ca.1709 – 1783 Only private banks existed.
All had the right to issue notes.

1783 – 1824 Bank of Ireland & private banks
1824 – 1921 Commercial Joint Stock Bank Issues
Private bank issues largely ceased by 1845

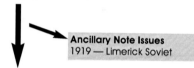

Ancillary Note Issues
1919 — Limerick Soviet

6 Dec 1921 — Ireland partitioned into the Irish Free State and Northern Ireland
Commercial Bank Issues 1921 – 1928

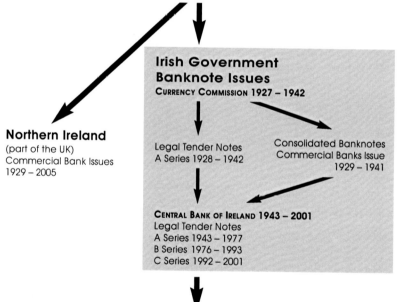

Irish Government Banknote Issues

CURRENCY COMMISSION 1927 – 1942

Northern Ireland
(part of the UK)
Commercial Bank Issues
1929 – 2005

Legal Tender Notes
A Series 1928 – 1942

Consolidated Banknotes
Commercial Banks Issue
1929 – 1941

CENTRAL BANK OF IRELAND 1943 – 2001
Legal Tender Notes
A Series 1943 – 1977
B Series 1976 – 1993
C Series 1992 – 2001

Euro 2002
The Republic of Ireland joins the Euro.
01.01.2002 — Euro notes replace the Irish Pound

Contents

The Background to Irish Banknote Issues from 1709

Old Banknotes — British Rule

Weak Banks and a Stagnant Economy

Banks first appeared in Ireland towards the end of the 17th century. The first reference to a bank in Irish law was in an act of 1709 which permitted bills of exchange to be made payable to the bearer rather than to a named individual. The Irish economy had great restrictions placed upon it by the English government in the late 18th and early 19th centuries. Ireland had a deflationary economy during this period, with a constant outflow of investment funds, mostly to Britain, largely by way of absentee landlords.

Numerous small so-called private banks were formed and went bust, mostly in Dublin, but also in Cork, Belfast, Waterford, Limerick and Clonmel. All Irish banks were permitted to issue their own banknotes, which were subject to a government stamp duty. Private banks at this time were prohibited by law from having more than six partners by an act of 1756, which also required all of the partners of the bank to be named on every banknote. Additionally bankers were prohibited by this act from engaging in trade involving import or export. These restrictions helped to keep private banks small and weak, and the economy suffered as a result.

The first attempt to redress the situation came with the foundation of the Bank of Ireland as a result of a petition to Parliament for an institution which would stimulate the Irish economy. The Bank was established by Royal Charter on 10 May 1783 and in return for a substantial loan to the Government it was granted the sole right of banknote issue in Ireland, except for private banks of six partners or less, and was to be banker to the Government. The bank was essentially a Central Bank, and was founded along the lines of The Bank of England and The Bank of Scotland, both of which had been created for a similar purpose. The bank commenced business on 25 June 1783, and proceeded to issue banknotes.

It was after the suspension of cash payments (i.e. gold) in 1797, due to England's need for gold to finance its wars on the continent, that banking and banknotes became more widespread in Ireland. This led to the growth of private banks, most of which issued their own notes.

The number of banks paying stamp duty on their notes was 11 in 1799. This had risen to 41 by 1803. By 1820 there were approximately 28 banks in the country. The Bank of Ireland provided a stable currency for Dublin and its surrounding areas, which allowed the Dublin private banks to concentrate their activities on banking rather than note issue. The presence of the Bank of Ireland had a stabilising influence on these small banks.

Three new private banks were founded in Belfast city around 1808–1809: Gordon's, Montgomery's and Tennant's. They were to lay the foundations of future banking in Ulster. Each of the three banks opened a number of agencies throughout Ulster, and by 1826 there were 16 towns in the province with one or more agencies of these banks. The three banks were closely linked to the emerging industrial base in Ulster and provided a stable, reliable banknote issue.

In 1820, the rest of the country outside of Dublin and Ulster had little industry, and was served by just 14 banks plus one agency issuing notes. The banking crisis of May–June 1820 in which 7 of these banks folded within a two-week period, fatally wounded confidence in the paper money issues of the country private banks in the South, with about 80% of the total note circulation eventually proving to be worthless. Of the remaining banks, all but one had closed by 1829. This last bank, Delacour's, finally closed in 1835.

All but one of the Dublin banks were supported by the Bank of Ireland with emergency loans during the 1820 crisis. This enabled them to survive demands for payment on their notes. The Northern banks were supported strongly by local industry, and required only a minor degree of assistance from the Bank of Ireland. However, the banking system in the rest of the country had been more or less left to its fate and allowed to collapse, due to a combination of sluggishness and disinterest on the part of the Bank of Ireland. Help when it did arrive was too little and too late. After lobbying by Cork merchants, the Bank of Ireland was authorised by Parliament to instigate a loan scheme to bail out suffering businesses in the South of the country. Over the course of the following few years, this alleviated much of the distress businesses were having in this region due to the banking crisis. Almost all of these loans were repaid in full.

For most of the 18th and early 19th centuries, there was a constant shortage of silver coinage in Ireland. This encouraged the widespread use of small notes, which were issued in varying denominations, by various merchants, businesses and private banks. Small notes, those with a value of less than £5, were issued in denominations of pence, shillings, guineas and pounds. Their issue and usage was largely uncontrolled, and disapproved of by government, which sought to restrict them in an effort to control the perceived over-issue of paper money in Ireland. The suspension of cash payments in 1797 exacerbated this, by prompting banks to increase their small note issues.

The Genesis of Irish Joint Stock Banking

Bank of Ireland regarded itself as a banker to the government and as a provider of loans on government security, and did not consider the provision of a currency for general use as part of its duties. It did not issue banknotes outside of Dublin until 1824. As such, there was a shortage of currency in the country outside of the Dublin and Ulster areas in the years prior to this.

Post bills, which for security in transit purposes were payable some days after issue, usually 7, but up to 21, tended also to be used as currency, as a compensation for the lack of banknotes in circulation. Bank of Ireland did not issue any small notes of denominations under £5 until the suspension of cash payments in 1797, which sucked a lot of coinage out of circulation. Some private banks did issue small notes, and greatly increased their issues after this. The Irish economy remained in a state of severe depression in 1820, with a large and growing population, little useful employment available, and famine always in the shadows.

By contrast, in 1820 Scotland had a sound banking system. In the rest of the UK, including Ireland, banks were forced by law to be small and weak. Scotland had been allowed to develop along different lines. The Bank of Scotland's special privileges had been abolished in 1716 and a strong joint stock banking system had been established. By 1826 there were three large multi-branch banks and 29 others in Scotland.

The need for reforms to the system outside of Scotland was recognised. The proposed changes were to be tested first in Ireland. In February 1821, discussions were opened with the Bank of Ireland on the restriction of its privileges, in an effort to stimulate development in the banking sector. These discussions led to the 1821 Act, which permitted banks of greater than six partners to issue notes outside of a radius of 50 miles of Dublin, a distance that appears to have been fixed arbitrarily. These changes were agreed with the Bank of Ireland in return for some minor extensions of the bank's business with the government. The bank retained a monopoly on note issue in Dublin.

There were a number of weaknesses in the act, which prevented it from having the effect of facilitating the creation of joint stock banks. Most significantly, no change had been made to the law governing the setting up of a bank (as laid out in the Act of 1756). All legal actions of the bank would still have to be conducted in the names of all the partners of that bank, a very cumbersome requirement. The act also specified that the partners must be resident in Ireland, thus precluding the injection of English capital into Irish banks.

The first lobbying for an improvement to the situation created by the 1821 Act came in March 1824, with a petition to Parliament on behalf of a group of Belfast businessmen and bankers seeking the repeal of the 1756 Act, so as to make the 1821 Act effective. The lack of strong banks in Ulster was beginning to stifle further industrial expansion. The petition was considered by parliament, and after a brief examination of the effect that the proposal would have on the Bank of Ireland, and the dismissal of that bank's objections to it, a bill was put forward which became law on June 17, as the Irish Banking Act, 1824. This act provided for banks of greater than six members, which could issue notes outside of a 50-mile radius of Dublin, provided that each bank registered annually, specifying the name of the officer under which it could sue and be sued, and the places of issue and of payment of its banknotes. The Northern Banking Company was founded directly as a result of the act. The new bank commenced business on 1 January 1825. It issued banknotes that were payable at the branch of issue and at the bank's head office in Belfast.

There were some ambiguities concerning the 1824 Act, the most significant of which was the question of English capital, not addressed at all in the act. A Newcastle on Tyne merchant, Thomas Joplin and a group of Irish MPs and others were promoting the idea of an Irish Provincial Banking Company, to serve mainly the southern part of the country, ignored by the existing banking system and still suffering from the effects of the banking crisis of 1820. The proposal for the new bank relied heavily on English capital, and the uncertainties regarding this point needed to be addressed. This resulted in the 1825 Act which resolved these problems by repealing the 1824 Act and specifically permitting members of banking partnerships to be resident anywhere in the UK.

By 1836, the Irish Banking Act, 1825 had led directly to the formation of five new Joint Stock note issuing banks; the Provincial (1825), the Belfast (1827), the Agricultural & Commercial (1834), the National (1835) and the Ulster (1836). The Belfast Bank was formed from existing private banks. Several other Joint Stock banks were formed which didn't issue their own notes, either because they chose not to do so, or because they were based in Dublin and were prohibited from doing so by law. The most important of these were the Hibernian (1825), and the Royal (1836). All but one of these banks drew on English capital as well as Irish. The Agricultural & Commercial drew solely on Irish capital. It was also the only Joint

Stock note issuing bank which failed, due largely to a lack of liquidity.

The next step was the unification of the Irish and English Pound. A proclamation of 1701 had fixed a value of twelve English pence equal to thirteen Irish pence, or a par rate of 8⅓% in favour of the English pound. This had effectively linked the two currencies. Prior to this, the Irish currency, such as it was, had floated on its own. With the suspension of cash payments in 1797, however, the actual rate fluctuated greatly on either side of this 8⅓% par rate, the link being in effect broken by the removal of the gold standard, producing a degree of instability as a result. The Act of Union, 1801 had abolished the Irish Parliament in Dublin and extended direct rule over Ireland by the English Parliament in London. Similarly the Assimilation of Currencies Act, 1825 now provided for the abolition of the separate Irish currency altogether on 6 January 1826. Thereafter only English Sterling circulated in Ireland. The gold standard was re-established on 1 May 1821. An Act of 1828 required banks to make their notes payable at the branch of issue, which was thereafter named on the notes along with the head office of the bank.

The Irish Banking Act, 1845

During the two decades from 1824 to 1844 a network of new banks and branches grew up across Ireland. The Bank of Ireland also established a branch network, opening its first branch in Cork in 1826. During this period, the Provincial and National in particular both grew rapidly in strength and sought to compete with and challenge the Bank of Ireland. An Act of 1830 authorised banks of greater than 6 partners to redeem their banknotes within 50 miles of Dublin, but not to re-issue them. This 20-year period saw the gradual erosion of the special privileges of the Bank of Ireland, which the bank sought to protect.

In the early 1840s, a major reform of British monetary thinking led to the 1844 Bank Charter Act in England, which placed limits on the quantity of notes that could be issued by any English bank, other than the Bank of England. The aim was to control the quantity of notes in circulation, in the interests of stability. Increases in the note issues of the Bank of England itself were to be fully backed by gold and silver reserves.

Following on from this new legislation in England, a consolidation of the system in Ireland took place with a new Irish regulatory act in 1844, which prohibited any new issuing banks and prevented the revival of a lapsed issuing bank. This paved the way for the 1845 Act. The Royal and Hibernian banks had sought the right to issue notes just prior to this act, but were prohibited from doing so by reason of their location in Dublin, despite the imminent abolition of the Bank of Ireland's privileges.

By the end of 1844, the Irish banks had 161 branches between them throughout Ireland. There followed a year later the Irish Banking Act 1845. It became law on 6 December 1845. This act was a substantial piece of legislation, the culmination of the "experiment" of the previous twenty-five years, and a reflection of recent changes in England. It fixed new regulations for note issues. Banks were allowed to issue an amount of money in their note issue up to a certified total, based upon their average issue over the previous 12-month period, their fiduciary issue, plus extra notes up to the value of their bullion holdings. It forbade any newly-formed bank from acquiring the right of note issue, and most importantly made all banks equal in terms of their operations, abolishing Bank of Ireland's special privileges. All banks of note issue were granted the right to issue and redeem banknotes throughout the entire country on an equal basis. Fractional notes and Guinea denominations were prohibited. This precluded notes of 25/- and 30/-, previously issued by banks.

Although there was friction between the Bank of Ireland and the other banks at times, particularly with the Provincial Bank of Ireland over government business being transacted in Provincial notes, the second half of the 19th century saw the growth of the six banks into a sophisticated co-operative banking system with the banks accepting each other's banknotes.

Several other Joint Stock Banks were formed after 1845, but were precluded from acquiring the right of note issue under the 1845 act. The most important of these was the Munster & Leinster Bank, founded in 1885. It was the only Joint Stock bank founded in this period which survived in business intact to the 20th century.

Irish Independence
and the Partition of Ireland

In the early 20th century politics was to intervene and have a major influence on Irish banking and note issues. The Rising of 1916 against British rule lead to the war of independence in 1919. The war resulted in a treaty, signed on 6 December 1921, which provided for the partition of the 32-county island into the 26-county Irish Free State and the 6-county Northern Ireland, which remained part of the UK. This was to have a huge effect on the banking system and on banknote circulation. The constitution of the Irish Free State came into force on 6 December 1922. From this date, the Irish Free State arguably became independent of the British Empire.

Under the provisions of the 1845 Bankers Ireland Act, the Irish banks were required to secure all notes in circulation in excess of their fiduciary issue by an equal amount of gold and silver coin, such that the silver did not exceed one quarter of the gold in value. As a result of the emergency situation created by the outbreak of World War I, the Currency and Banknotes Act of 5 August 1914 provided for the creation of Treasury notes, which were to take the place of gold coin in circulation. These notes also circulated in Ireland. In 1920, these were the only Legal Tender Notes circulating in Ireland. Irish banknotes had been made legal tender in 1914, due to the war situation, with this status then being revoked at the end of 1919. The 1914 Act allowed the banks to substitute British currency notes for bullion, as cover for their excess note issues. All circulating notes, fiduciary and secured, were subject to a stamp duty of 7/- per £100 (0.35%) per annum.

Two Irish Currencies

In 1928, the Sterling unit of currency was the Pound, with main subdivisions as follows: One Pound = 20 Shillings, One Shilling = 12 Pennies, 1 Penny = 4 Farthings. This system prevailed until decimalisation in 1969 when the Pound was divided into 100 pence. One Shilling then became equal to 5 pence. The Irish currency was based on the exact same structure as that of Sterling and was linked to Sterling on a par basis from its inception in 1928 up to Ireland's entry into the ERM on 13 March 1979, when the link was broken and the Irish Pound became linked loosely to a basket of EC currencies. Because of the link to Sterling, Ireland adopted a similar decimal currency at the same time as Britain. Sterling always circulated freely in Ireland in small quantities until the termination of the link.

Sterling had been legal tender in Ireland since 1826. After Irish independence in 1921 the banknotes of the Irish banks continued to circulate throughout the island of Ireland, as did English currency. The British and Irish Governments had made an informal agreement in 1923 to divide the stamp duty on circulating notes as follows: the Government of Northern Ireland would collect the duty on banknotes of the Northern, Ulster and Belfast Banks, whilst the Government of the Irish Free State would collect the duty on the notes of the Bank of Ireland, the Provincial and National banks. This measure served to avoid double taxation of the banks' note issues.

However, during the 1920s, the need for a distinctive Irish currency and an authority to control its issue became apparent. A Banking Commission was appointed on 8 March 1926 by the Minister for Finance, Ernest Blythe, to study the matter. It sat for nine months, issuing four interim reports and one final report. The Banking Commission recommended the establishment of a currency commission in the Irish Free State, to issue and regulate a new currency, the Saorstát Pound. The Commission's recommendations lead to the 1927 Currency Act.

The currency circulating in Ireland changed radically with the provisions of the 1927 act. The Currency Commission was created and commenced the issue of Legal Tender Notes in 1928. In 1929, the Associated (Joint Stock) Banks' issues on the island of Ireland were split into Consolidated Banknotes, controlled by the Currency Commission in the Irish Free State, and a new issue for Northern Ireland.

The agreement on the collection of duty on notes continued up to the establishment of the Currency Commission and the intention of replacing all notes of the banks with a new issue of consolidated notes in the Irish Free State on an appointed day. The duty on existing (to become old) notes became a bone of contention at this point. There was considerable debate between the two governments over how to divide up the responsibility for the banknotes already in circulation. Originally it was proposed by Joseph Brennan that the notes in their entirety of the banks headquartered in Dublin (Bank of Ireland) and London (Provincial and National) would be apportioned to the Irish Free State, with those of the banks headquartered in Belfast (Northern and Ulster) being apportioned to Northern Ireland. The Belfast Banking Co. having withdrawn from operations outside of Northern Ireland automatically had 100% of its notes apportioned to Northern Ireland.

Mr. Brennan's suggestion was found to be unacceptable to the British Government, and instead it was agreed that the outstanding notes of the five banks operating in both jurisdictions were to be divided in relation to the bank's operations in each. The percentages allocated to the Irish Free State were as follows:

Bank of Ireland	87%
The National Bank	95%
The Northern Bank	28%
The Provincial Bank of Ireland	82%
The Ulster Bank	42%

This made up 71% of the total circulation in Pounds of the five banks.

For the purpose of taxation on note issues in the Irish Free State, the proportion of old notes appertaining to the State which were still outstanding on the appointed day, 6 May 1929, for each of the banks, were counted as part of the consolidated issue for that bank and would be taxed at 1.5% per annum, the same rate as applied to consolidated notes. A higher tax was to be levied on any old notes extant greater than half of the bank's allocation of Consolidated Banknotes. These old notes outstanding which exceeded the limit permitted would be subject to a tax of 3% for the first year and 5% p.a. thereafter. A provision was also fixed for a sliding taxation scale of 5%, rising to a maximum of 10.5% p.a. for an extraordinary issue of Consolidated Banknotes above a bank's limit.

THE BACKGROUND TO IRISH BANKNOTE ISSUES

The Bankers' Northern Ireland Bill fixed the provisions for the creation of the Northern Ireland Issue in place of the all-Ireland issue of the Irish banks. It became law on 2 July 1928. A provision of the Act was that it would not come into effect until after the appointed day for the currency changeover, a date to be fixed by the Currency Commission. This created the curious situation in that a piece of British legislation would not become law until an Act of Parliament was passed outside of British jurisdiction. New fiduciary limits were fixed for the banks based upon their size and assets within Northern Ireland, with a requirement of security in British Treasury and Bank of England notes for any notes in circulation in excess of these limits. However, the provisions of the act made it clear that the entire number of notes in circulation exceeding the fiduciary limit, whether appertaining to the Irish Free State or to Northern Ireland, would have to be backed by security in British currency. This requirement, when enforced, would place a significant hardship on the banks for as long as their own old notes circulated in the Irish Free State after the appointed day. They would be required to be backed by British security, whilst also being treated as consolidated banknotes by the Currency Commission, and taxed accordingly by the Irish Government.

The bill was amended to allow for a period of grace after the appointed day for the banks to have time to reduce their circulation to the new fiduciary limits before the requirements for securing notes were to come into effect. This double burden rapidly decreased as the old notes of the banks were withdrawn and replaced by Consolidated notes.

The double tax burden did not disappear, however, in the case of dead notes, those which would never be presented for payment due to being irretrievably lost or destroyed. Joseph Brennan identified this question early on as being a major bone of contention. In 1929, the banks sought to write off a certain portion of their notes as dead, and cease payment of stamp duty on them. This was not permitted by either government at the time. The question of dead notes was never resolved. Section 40 of the Central Bank Act, 1942, provided for the conditional possibility of the writing off of dead notes at the request of the bank concerned, should the request be deemed to be appropriate. According to Moynihan in his book *"Currency and Central Banking in Ireland 1922 – 1960"*, as at 1974 no such request had ever been made[1]. Subsequent to this date information is not available in relation to this interesting topic.

The Banknotes
The banknote issues of all of the joint Stock Banks except the Bank of Ireland were of a generally similar standard design and were printed in England. The Bank of Ireland's notes were different, and from early on were printed by the bank itself in Dublin. There were three major design changes, the last being ca.1838 with the introduction of the classic design featuring a row of heads along the top of each note. This basic design then remained unchanged for 120 years. Banknotes of the Northern and Belfast banks were always printed on both sides. Those of the other banks were uniface, with reverse printing being introduced only in the early 20th century, as follows: Bank of Ireland (1922), Provincial (1920), National (1924), Ulster (1935).

The 1828 Act, which became operative on 1 April 1829, required banknotes to be payable at the branch of issue, and therefore the place name, usually the name of the town where the issuing branch was located had to be stated on each note from this time on. This was a somewhat cumbersome printing process.

The earliest appearance of the multi-branch banknote designs, with all of the branches listed on each note was around 1850 on some notes of the Bank of Ireland. All of the banks introduced multi-branch notes over the following two decades. The multi-branch notes of the three Northern banks listed two main offices, Belfast and Dublin, although Belfast retained head office status. The other banks listed only Dublin as the principal office of payment.

The multi-branch banknote designs appear to have been a device to facilitate a reduction in the costs of printing, enabling more generic note designs to be used. As new branches were established, they were added to notes, sometimes as overprints. The plates of each denomination were re-engraved periodically to include new branches in the main branch listings. This system has produced many branch sub-varieties for some of the banks.

The Banknotes (Ireland) Act 1920 removed the requirement on the banks to redeem their notes at the branch of issue, requiring payment only at the principal office of each bank. It was therefore no longer necessary to state the branch of issue and payment on the note, and branch listings disappeared from notes of all the banks. Thus, the multi-branch banknotes came to an end. The issuing banks all produced new note issues as a result of the 1920 Act. Most of the banks had already begun to reduce the size of their £1 notes. The National Bank, in a very modernist move, made all of its notes smaller sized. Small-sized notes of the National Bank, Provincial Bank and Bank of Ireland appear both with and without branch listings. Bank of Ireland introduced a new series in 1922, with all denominations being printed on both sides. £1 notes of the Northern,

---

1.   *"Currency and Central Banking in Ireland 1922 – 1960"*, Moynihan, Dr. M., page 166, Gill & Macmillan and The Central Bank of Ireland, 1975.

Provincial and Ulster banks were also reduced in size, with the Provincial £1 notes being printed on both sides for the first time. All denominations of the National's post multi-branch notes were printed on both sides and were all of a similar size.

Northern Ireland Issue

With the exception of the National Bank, the Belfast Banking Co., and the Provincial Bank, each of which produced completely new designs for their Northern Ireland issues, all of the other banks' Northern Ireland notes were almost identical in design to the previous all-Ireland old note issues. The principal differences were a new serial prefixing system and Belfast being substituted as the office of payment in place of Dublin.

The Northern and Ulster banks each produced an initial issue of overprinted notes on an all-Ireland design, in order to use up stocks of previously printed notes. The Ulster Bank's overprinted series consisted of £1 notes only and were rapidly used up, The Northern Bank overprinted series was more extensive, spanning across most denominations. It appears that the £50 and £100 note overprints were issued periodically up to the end of the 1960s. They are relatively easy to obtain.

Irish Government Banknotes
Currency Commission Legal Tender Notes

The Currency Act 1927 resulted from the Banking Commission's recommendations. It became law on 20 August 1927. The Act provided for the establishment of a Currency Commission as an independent non-political body which would control and manage the new Irish currency, the "Saorstát Pound".

The Currency Commission was granted power to issue Legal Tender banknotes in denominations of 10/- (Ten Shillings), £1, £5, £10, £20, £50, and £100. The first issue date of each denomination of these notes was 10.9.28. They entered circulation on this date of issue.

In accordance with the Banking Commission's recommendations, the Saorstát Pound was linked to Sterling to ensure the former's stability, and was exchangeable at par with Sterling, though the Irish currency was not legal tender in the UK.

Currency Commission Consolidated Banknotes

With regard to the fact that some of the commercial banks had their own note issues in use, all of the joint stock circulation banks were admitted as share-holding banks (known as the Associated Banks) of the Currency Commission. Thus, the right of note issue of the commercial banks was retained, though at reduced levels and with the inclusion of a greater number of banks. The Consolidated Banknote issue was created to facilitate this purpose.

These notes were not Legal Tender, but payable in Legal Tender Notes on demand. The notes were of a standard overall design differing only in the title of the bank of issue. The initial total aggregate of the Consolidated Banknotes was not to exceed £6,000,000 in value, with the outstanding amount of old notes of

Consolidated Banknotes

The figures for the amount allocated to each of the Associated Banks were as follows	
The Bank of Ireland Ltd.	£1,760,000*
The Hibernian Bank Ltd.	£439,000
The Munster & Leinster Bank Ltd.	£852,000
The National Bank Ltd.	£1,365,000
The Northern Bank Ltd.	£243,000
The Provincial Bank of Ireland Ltd.	£649,000
The Royal Bank of Ireland Ltd.	£273,000
The Ulster Bank Ltd.	£419,000
Total	£6,000,000

*Including £77,000 originally allocated to the state-owned National Land Bank.

Northern Ireland Issue

Fiduciary Issue of the banks	Old Notes 1923	Northern Ireland 1928
The Bank of Ireland Ltd.	£3,738,428	£410,000
The Belfast Banking Company Ltd.	£243,000	£244,000
The National Bank Ltd.	£852,269	£120,000
The Northern Bank Ltd.	£281,611	£290,000
The Provincial Bank of Ireland Ltd.	£927,667	£220,000
The Ulster Bank Ltd.	£311,079	£350,000
Total	£6,354,494	£1,634,000

the banks included in this total. The appointed day for their introduction was 6 May 1929.

Three banks, the Hibernian, the Munster & Leinster, and the Royal, issued banknotes bearing their own names for the first time on 6 May 1929.

The existence of the Consolidated Banknote issue is a testament to the power held by the commercial banks at the time and the fact that they provided the country with a currency. However, it was always envisaged that the State would eventually remove the right of note issue from these banks. The Consolidated Banknote issue served as a means to this end.

The Central Bank of Ireland

A second Banking Commission was appointed in November 1934, to consider the situation of banking within the Irish State. It published its final report in 1938. The most important of its recommendations was that a Central Bank with greater powers be established in place of the Currency Commission. Also, it recommended a cessation of the right of note issue for the Associated banks, which would mean the end of the Consolidated Banknote issue.

The Central Bank of Ireland Act, 1942, resulted from the recommendations of the second Banking Commission. It terminated the Currency Commission, transferring its assets, liabilities, and responsibilities to the new authority, the Central Bank of Ireland, which formally came into being on 1 February 1943. The basic design of Legal Tender Notes was not altered except for the title of the new Issuing Authority, "The Central Bank of Ireland" which replaced that of "Currency Commission Ireland" on the top of each banknote.

The issue of Consolidated Banknotes was terminated on 31 December 1953. The amounts of Consolidated notes in use by the associated banks had always been less than the permitted total, due to old notes being outstanding. The quantity of Consolidated Banknotes in existence on 31 December 1953 was £620,191. This was considerably less than the total permitted aggregate at the time, which was £1,299,000.

The Associated Banks permitted aggregate was gradually reduced over three year periods. It reached zero on 31 December 1956. As of that date, the Central Bank of Ireland had sole right of note issue, and all of the Consolidated Banknotes were to be withdrawn from circulation by 1 January 1957, when the Central Bank of Ireland would acquire responsibility for the outstanding notes.

On 31 March 1954, six of the Associated Banks paid amounts equalling their total outstanding Consolidated notes, including old notes, to the Central Bank. This totalled £400,422. The remaining two banks (the Bank of Ireland and the Provincial) paid up the total amount of their outstanding notes by the end of 1956, totalling £140,399. The Central Bank of Ireland continues to redeem the Consolidated Banknotes at their face value as they are presented.

1976 saw the introduction of B Series Legal Tender Notes, which replaced the A Series on a phased basis, a process completed when the B Series £50 note entered circulation in 1982. The £100 denomination was not replaced and the A Series £100 remained in use.

Sixteen years later, in 1992, the C Series Legal Tender Notes were introduced. The new design replaced the B Series over the following four years, culminating in the introduction of a new £100 note in 1996.

The End of the Irish Currency

On 31 December 1998 the EU single currency, the Euro, came into being when eleven (Austria, Belgium, Germany, Finland, France, Ireland, Italy, Luxembourg, Portugal, Spain and The Netherlands) of the fifteen EU countries merged their currencies, by locking their exchange rates with respect to each other (A twelfth, Greece joined later). The Irish Pound became locked at a value of 1 Euro equal to IR£0.787564. Euro banknotes and coins replaced national currencies in circulation on 1 January 2002. The European Central Bank has control over the Euro, and the Issuing Authorities of the member countries became offices of the European Central Bank.

There is no fixed date for the demonetisation of old Irish banknotes, and all notes issued by the Joint Stock banks and the Currency Commission and Central Bank of Ireland are redeemable at their face value.

Notes issued in Northern Ireland by the Irish banks are regulated by the Bank of England and are as yet not part of the Euro zone currencies.

Irish banknotes outstanding

The total amount of A Series notes outstanding on 31 March 1929 was £6,557,998. This amount had risen to just over £7 million by 31 March 1930 and remained in this region until around 1935, when the amount in circulation began to rise steadily, both in response to an improving economy and to the steady decline of the amount of Consolidated notes in circulation. By 31 March 1943, just after the foundation of the Central Bank of Ireland, the total amount outstanding was £23,061,356 10/-.

The total outstanding issues of the five banks in 1929 amounted to approximately £9,205,000. Of this, £6,525,719 was apportioned to the Irish Free State. Approximately £5,000,000 of this had been withdrawn from circulation by 31 March 1932. By 31 March 1971, the total outstanding figure was £775,450, with £628,981 appertaining to the Republic of Ireland. The total outstanding on 30 September 2001 was approximately £628,000. A significant proportion of these banknotes may be assumed to be dead notes which will never be presented for payment, including presumably those in collections.

The total amount of Consolidated banknotes outstanding on 30 September 2001 was £105,250. Total Legal Tender Notes outstanding on 31 December 2001, the day before the Euro entered circulation, was approximately £3,420,725,000.

Determining the relative rarity of Consolidated banknotes.

Ploughman notes Dead and buried?

With regard to the Consolidated notes, the question of dead notes has been a mater of considerable speculation over the past thirty years or so. Speculation is all that has occurred, it would appear, with little in the way of actual observation.

Derek Young made a lot of progress in the 1970s and 1980s in his Guide to the Currency of Ireland books, and in Irish Numismatics, in recording and publishing information on both the Lavery and Ploughman series. He had the assistance of some of the leading collectors and researchers of Irish notes of the day. With the assistance of some of these researchers and other new-comers (myself included!), I was able to greatly extend the information on Lavery notes, and virtually completed the data on B and C Series notes by the time my book, Irish Banknotes was published in 1999. This was helped a lot by monetary inflation between the 1980 and 2000, making possible access to the higher denomination notes in bulk. Thus, Lavery £20, £50, and £100 notes were recorded in quantity during this period. A significant number of examples of unrecorded dates have been added since then, and the project continues. Several updates of these additions have been published thus far. Eventually, all of these data will be posted on-line.

Ploughman notes, however, were always scarce. They were not available from circulation to study in large quantities. So people took to guessing—some guesses have been more educated than others—and a couple of works were published based on the guesswork. All have their shortcomings to some degree.

Gibb's analysis (IN, No. 65, Sept–Oct, 1978, p203) which attempts to estimate the relative rarity of Ploughman notes is flawed and simplistic in that it does not take into account the usage factor over time of the notes when they were in circulation in the period 1929 to 1944. During this time soiled and damaged notes of earlier dates were being replaced by fresh notes of later dates. This would obviously weigh the rarity in favour of earlier notes, and therefore earlier signatures when there was more than one signature for a bank in a given denomination. This is ignored by Gibb's analysis. Thus, for example, he got a completely inaccurate answer of

1:1 for the relative rarity of Northern Knox signature £1 notes to Northern Stewart signature £1 notes. The whole system of analysis is flawed in this article.

The PMI analysis (PMI, p456, 457) into the surviving numbers of notes is also flawed by the taking of a likely too low guess of 10% of dead notes as having survived to be available to collectors. This guess clearly gives an incorrect answer for the number of survivors of some of the denominations. The most striking of these is the Hibernian £10 note (stated at 18 notes), a medium scarcity note of which there were 14 on offer at a fair in Dublin in 2010; and the Ulster £10 (stated at 8 notes) being almost as rare as the Northern (stated at 7 notes), which it obviously isn't. Conclusion, the authors didn't look at enough notes.

So, whilst neither of these articles appears to be based on a rigorous study of the notes over time, both are based on the Central Bank's available data on the number of notes outstanding, and on an analysis which ignores some of the the facts of what is actually out there. Neither has taken into account the numbers of notes actually observed in the field, or the nature of stashes, which generally favour higher denomination notes, facts necessary to control for error in the analysis.

The known surviving notes need to be considered in any relative rarity analysis of the notes. My own brief analysis of relative rarity, published in 1999 (IB, p24) was based on observation. It is also flawed, in that no analysis can take into account what *might turn up* subsequently, either from source stashes of old notes, or out of the general collector pool as time progresses, and more and more notes are recorded. This is exactly what happened with regard to the Hibernian Bank, Hodges signature £1 note (IB, p163). This signature, with one recorded date, was very rare back in 1999, and I gave it 3 stars for rarity, the same as the Northern Bank Stewart signature £1. Large numbers of Hodges £1 notes have turned up subsequently, all with that same date. Many of them are nicer grades, with a lot of those being near UNC. It is now by far the most common date for the Hibernian Bank, and the signature is no longer rare. Hence the Hodges £1 note subsequently was reduced to one star rarity in an earlier edition of this book. This is despite the fact that there were approximately 10 times as many Campbell £1 notes (prefixes 01HA-22HA) as there were Hodges (prefixes 23HA-24HA 009576) notes. It also supports the notion that the earlier date (and signature) notes were retired as they wore out in favour of later date (and signature) notes—common sense, but nice to see evidence for it.

The erosion of the rarity of the Hodges £1 demonstrates neatly the flaw in the Gibb analysis (not taking into account the usage factor), and in the PMI analysis (not looking adequately at the number of notes out there), and in my analysis (not being able to take into account what may turn up subsequently).

The dynamic nature of the changing relative rarity of the Ploughman notes, and the relatively small number of notes out there, point to the absolute need to determine this rarity from observation alone, relying on the sparse background statistics only as a guideline.

Over longer periods of time new notes to the census which turn up will tend to average out over all of the banks and denominations to reflect the true relative rarity of each note with respect to others. Occasionally, there may be a glut of one particular note, as was the case with National £5 notes where a known hoard of at least 100 notes in sequence leaked and then poured onto the market. The broader rarity of the banks relative to each other has remained generally the same over the past 15 years of the study, though notes of the Hibernian Bank have become less scarce than they were relative to other banks for all of the denominations.

So how do we examine the facts available and come up with an accurate answer? First, we have the statistical information from the Central Bank. Next, we have a pool of known extant notes in collections. which we need to take into account when considering the statistical data—that means looking at a lot of notes over a long period of time. This is all we need for relative rarity. The more banknotes we look at, the more robust our conclusions will be, especially in the case where a hoard of similar notes turns up.

It is likely that the only statistics of banknotes outstanding that are relevant to research on relative rarity would be those after around 1980, when every Ploughman note was kept, rather than only those in better grade as was the case formerly. It can be seen from the 1984 and 2001 figures that the amount of notes

being turned in over the intervening period of 17 years or so had fallen to a small trickle, at £102 face value.

Consolidated notes outstanding.

Oct, 1971: £111895 (CBN, D. Young, p11)
Mar, 1972: £110,693 (CBN, D. Young, p11)
Aug, 1984: £105,352 (Central Bank, as published in
            Irish Numismatics, cited in PMI, p457)
Sept, 2001: £105,250 (Central Bank)

Relative rarity of Consolidated notes

Table 1 presents the relative rarity of each denomination when compared to other notes of that denomination. It is based on 15 years' observation and recording of the notes. There are so many Bank of Ireland £1 notes that it is necessary to go beyond a scale of 1 to 10 to represent them! A much more rigorous analysis of these data will be published in due course.

One noteworthy point is the scarcity of the Bank of Ireland £10—always an uncommon note—which has maintained its relative rarity since I first started looking at these notes around 1996. Royal £10 notes have moved closer to the Ulster, and Hibernian £10 notes have become much less scarcer than they were.

Banknote Census Project
Recording an example of every date

On *www.irishpapermoney.com* there is a list of all the dates of A Series and Consolidated banknotes and an image of a note of every recorded date of these Series is presented, though there are a few recorded banknote dates for which images have not yet become available for illustration—if you have one please send a scan of it! This gallery is being extended to include images of B and C Series notes also.

Table 1: Relative rarity of Consolidated Banknotes, based on observation								
	BoI	Hib	M&L	Nat	Nor	PBI	RB	UB
£1	14	6	8	9	1	7	5	3
£5	7	6	7	10	1	6	3	3
£10	4	6	10	8	1	6	4	4

Even the rarest notes can turn up in stereo!

14

A Series notes

Thus far, examples of the following dates have yet to be recorded for A Series banknotes:

10/-	15.5.45.
£5	6.4.37, 24.5.51, 15.9.55.
£10	16.3.33.
£20	5.4.43, 7.6.43, 4.11.43, 10.1.44, 17.10.45, 13.12.45, 16.1.46, 23.7.47, 26.9.47, 3.10.47, 16.3.48, 21.7.48, 7.9.48, 14.10.48, 26.11.48, 7.3.49, 19.5.49, 17.11.49, 18.3.50, 14.9.50, 22.5.51.
£50	5.4.43, 2.7.43, 29.1.46, 26.2.46, 22.5.46, 18.6.47, 26.7.47, 16.5.49, 4.9.50.
£100	20.12.37, 30.3.43, 20.11.47.

Most of the £20 and £50 note dates in this list are not rare, relatively speaking.

Consolidated notes

Leaving aside the 1940–41-dated Extraordinary Issue (EI) notes, very few of the Consolidated note dates remain to be recorded as follows:

Hibernian	£1: 1.5.34; £5: 13.9.39; £10: 24.7.39.
M & L	£1: 24.8.32.
National	£1: 3.7.34; £5: 29.1.31, 16.9.39; £10: 5.12.31, 31.7.39.
Northern	£1: 9.10.39; £5: 15.9.39.
Provincial	£1: 5.9.36; £5: 19.3.39.
Royal	£5: 21.9.39.
Ulster	£1: 7.1.31; £5: 11.9.39.

Some of these were almost certainly never issued as they were part of the Extraordinary Issue (all the late 1939 dates). However, some EI notes have appeared (M & L £1, 6.2.40; M & L £5, 22.9.39; PBI £10, 17.7.39 (several in sequence) so others may do so in the future.

Readers with examples of any notes of these dates might like to send details of serial numbers to: *lists@irishpapermoney.com* with a scan of the note if possible.

A Note on ETO Code (War Code) Banknotes.

As of 1 April 2014, an example of each of the dates of all the denominations of ETO code notes has been recorded except for three £20 note dates: 5.4.43, 4.11.43 and 10.1.44. This is tantalisingly close to a complete set!

The ETO code was an extra security feature, used to keep track of the Irish banknotes from the time of

their production in England to their being delivered safely to Ireland.

Contrary to what has been stated elsewhere (PMI, 2009, p406) there appears to be no evidence to support the notion that ETO codes on Types 4 and 5 Legal Tender Notes were added "*to identify those issues that the UK authorities would have refused to redeem*" had Ireland been invaded (presumably by the Germans). Perhaps this was the reason for the ETO codes, perhaps not, but currently the statement is speculative and does not come with any cited supporting evidence or references. The usage of the ETO codes was prescribed by the Irish government at the time, a fact for which there is documentary evidence.

Also, that £50 and £100 notes dated 1943 were produced during this period without ETO codes would tend to disprove the notion that the UK authorities had required the inclusion of the ETO codes on Irish banknotes for the stated reason. Besides, by June 1941, after the Battle of Britain had been won by the RAF, a German invasion of Ireland was even less likely than the notion of a German invasion of Britain. Why then continue ETO usage until 1944?

The usage of ETO codes on Irish notes commenced in September 1940 when the Blitz started and ceased after the D-Day landings in 1944, when German bombing of London had stopped.

A general request for research assistance from the collecting community!

As already mentioned, a survey of Ploughman and rarer Lavery notes has been underway for the past 15 years. We need **your help** with this now to improve the quality of the data and the accuracy of the results!

Readers are requested to help by sending scans of Ploughman notes and the following A Series Lavery notes to *lists@irishpapermoney.com* to help in filling in missing information.

£10:	1928, 1933.
£20:	1928, 1943–1953.
£50:	1928, 1943–1960.
£100:	1928, 1943–1960.

Additionally, scans would be appreciated of notes missing from the irishpapermoney.com date list, here: http://www.irishpapermoney.com/a/date/a0dates.html

---

References cited in text.

1. CBN: "*Guide to the Currency of Ireland Consolidated Bank Notes 1929 – 1941*", Young D., Stagecast Pub., Dublin, 1977.
1. IN: "*Irish numismatics*" magazine, Young D, Ed., 1969–1984.
3. "*Irish Banknotes – Irish Government Paper Money from 1928*", Mac Devitt M., 1999.
4. PMI: "*Paper Money of Ireland*", Blake & Calloway, 2009.

The Irish Joint Stock Banks of Note Issue

Twelve Banks

There follows a brief introduction to the Joint Stock banks that issued banknotes in Ireland. Nine Joint Stock Banks were in existence in Ireland when the country was partitioned into The Irish Free State and Northern Ireland in 1922. Six of these banks had the right to issue their own banknotes, by virtue of the fact of their having been founded prior to the 1845 Act.

Other Joint Stock Banks were founded both before and after the 1845 Act. They either chose not to issue their own notes, or were prohibited from doing so. All of these other banks either failed or were taken over prior to 1929 by one of the surviving banks listed here.

The Belfast Banking Company restricted its operations to Northern Ireland only, leaving five note issuing banks, which along with the other three banks became the eight Associated Banks in the Irish Free State. All of these received the right to issue banknotes under the Consolidated banknote issue in 1929, whilst the Currency Commission, as the Issuing Authority, regulated banknote issue within the state and also issued its own series of Legal Tender Notes. It should be noted that The Bank of Ireland was by far the most powerful of the eight Associated Banks. All six of the banks which had the right to issue banknotes prior to partition continued to issue their own banknotes in Northern Ireland under the regulation of the Bank of England.

The Agricultural & Commercial Bank of Ireland 1834–1840

First proposed as the National Commercial Bank of Ireland, the Agricultural & Commercial Bank was founded by Thomas Mooney as a bank for farmers and smallholders. The bank opened its first branch in Nenagh on 1 November 1834. By 1839 it had 44 branches plus a non-branch head office in 4 College Green, Dublin. There was considerable rivalry between this bank and the National. The Agricultural issued two series of banknotes.

The bank was poorly organised, badly managed and incompetently run. It expanded too fast for its capabilities. It also opened branches in Ulster, a province already well served by strong banks which the Agricultural could not compete effectively against. However, its most critical shortcoming was its capital base. Unlike other Irish banks, one of its founding ideals had been that of an Irish bank for Ireland. Because of this it relied solely on Irish shareholders and had no English capital base to draw upon in times of crisis as did the other Irish banks. This was to prove fatal to the bank.

There was a run on the National and Agricultural banks in 1836 during a financial crisis at the time. Although the National fared well, some of the branches of the Agricultural stopped payment on its notes in November 1836 due to a lack of readily available cash. Although it had failed in liquidity, the bank was, nonetheless, solvent and it resumed payment on its notes on 23 January 1837.

Following continual difficulties in liquidity and much acrimony, the Agricultural & Commercial again suspended payment on 19 April 1840. The bank was not bailed out by the Bank of Ireland and it never resumed operations. Its debts were finally paid off by ca.1851.

The Bank of Ireland 1783

The Bank of Ireland was established by Royal Charter on 10 May 1783, by a group of over 200 Irish businessmen, land owners and clergymen, to stimulate and regulate the Irish economy and to provide it with a stable banknote currency. The bank was granted the sole right of banknote issue in Ireland except for Private banks of six partners or less, and was to be banker to the government. It commenced business on 25 June 1783, and proceeded to issue banknotes. The Bank of Ireland was essentially similar to a modern Central Bank of sorts, and was founded along the lines of The Bank of England and The Bank of Scotland.

The bank's first premises was in Mary's Abbey, Dublin, purchased in 1784. In 1802 the bank purchased the old Irish Parliament House, College Green, Dublin, vacant since the Act of Union, and located its head office there in 1808. One of the most attractive buildings in the city of Dublin, the former parliament House has been the bank's flagship branch ever since and was its head office for over a century.

The creation of Joint Stock banks of note issue as a result of the 1824 Act, and the subsequent erosion of the Bank of Ireland's special privileges, leading up to their abolition with the 1845 Act, provided for the effective reduction in status of the bank to that of a Joint Stock bank. It was as a result of this levelling of the rules that the bank felt it necessary to expand into the country and compete with the other banks by establishing its own branches, the first of which was opened in March 1825, in Cork. Prior to the 1824 Act, the Bank of Ireland had largely ignored the country outside of Dublin.

The bank, however, still had significance, in that its assets and prestige far exceeded that of any other bank, and its notes were considered to be as good as gold.

With Irish independence in 1921, the Bank of Ireland aspired to become the currency regulatory authority for the new Irish Free State, even though its ethos at the time would not have favoured Irish independence. Although it failed in these aspirations, the bank served as an important part of the Currency Commission's currency distribution network.

The Bank of Ireland printed notes under the Consolidated Banknote system from 1929 to 1939, as well as its own Northern Ireland issue. It continues to issue banknotes in Northern Ireland to this day. The Bank exists to the present day, having taken over both the Hibernian Bank and the National Bank.

The Belfast Banking Company 1827–1970

The Belfast Banking Co. was formed with 337 shareholders on 2 July 1827, by a merger of the then two remaining private banks in Belfast, Batt's (The Belfast Bank, in business since 1808) and Tennant's (The Commercial Bank). It was organised on similar lines to the Northern Banking Co. and commenced business on 1 August 1827. In 1917 its share capital was sold to the London Joint City & Midland Bank Ltd.

The Belfast Banking Co. remained mostly an "Ulster" bank, and had relatively few branches outside the Province, not opening an office in Dublin until 1892. In 1923 the bank sold to the Royal Bank of Ireland the 20 branches which it had in the newly-formed Irish Free State. Thus the bank became the only one of the Irish Joint Stock banks to operate solely in Northern Ireland. A new series of banknotes was produced in 1922 for issue in Northern Ireland only. It appears that Belfast Banking Co. notes were always printed on both sides.

In 1965 The Northern Bank was taken over by the Midland Bank, which already owned the Belfast Bank. The Belfast was then merged into the Northern in 1970.

The Hibernian Bank 1825–1958

The Bank was founded as The Hibernian Joint Stock and Annuity Company in April 1825. It opened on 20 June 1825 with 1063 shareholders, many of them London based. Its foundation by a group of Dublin businessmen was in response to anti-Catholic discrimination by Bank of Ireland. It changed its name later to The Hibernian Bank. The bank aimed itself primarily at the Dublin business community.

Bank of Ireland opposed any attempts by The Hibernian Bank to acquire the right to issue banknotes of its own. The Hibernian issued Tokens, engraved on stamped paper, signed and dated. Although legal, these were withdrawn following their opposition by Bank of Ireland. There have been unconfirmed reports of a Hibernian banknote issue dated 1825 or 1826.

In 1844, the Hibernian again tried unsuccessfully to obtain the right of note issue. Any further attempts to obtain the right to issue its own notes were prevented by the 1845 Act.

A large size Old Note. These banknotes are covered in detail in my earlier book *"Irish Paper Money 1783 – 2005"* and also more recently in much greater detail in *"Paper Money of Ireland"* by Blake and Calloway. I shall return to them in future books. There are also many illustrations of Old Notes on www.irishpapermoney.com

In 1885 the Hibernian Bank was reconstituted and the name changed to The Hibernian Bank Ltd. The Bank received the right to issue its own Banknotes in 1929, when it issued Consolidated Banknotes in the Irish Free State.

The Hibernian Bank was taken over by Bank of Ireland in 1958.

The Munster & Leinster Bank Ltd 1885–1966

The bank was established on 19 September 1885, to take over the business of the failed Munster Bank, mostly by shareholders of that bank.

It commenced business on 19 October 1885 in several of the premises of the former Munster Bank. Later the Munster & Leinster Bank purchased 35 out of 43 of the Munster Bank's former branches, including the Dublin and Cork premises. The Munster & Leinster Bank Ltd. issued its own banknotes for the first time in 1929, with the Consolidated Banknote issue.

In 1966, The Munster & Leinster Bank merged with The Provincial Bank of Ireland and The Royal Bank of Ireland to form Allied Irish Banks.

The National Bank Ltd 1835–1966

This bank was formed in 1834 in London by Daniel O'Connell and the Nationalist Party as The National Bank of Ireland. The deed of covenant was signed on 6 January 1835 by 249 shareholders. The first Branch opened in Carrick on Suir either on Monday 26 or Wednesday 28 January 1835 (history appears not to have recorded what the exact date was!). The Bank's first Governor was Daniel O'Connell, a fact which earned the Bank the nickname of The Liberator's Bank.

The bank aimed itself at farmers and at country business outside Dublin. It expanded its branch network rapidly, but refrained from moving into Ulster to any significant degree as the province was then well covered by banks. In 1856 the Bank's name was changed to The National Bank Ltd., as it commenced business in London.

The National Bank issued its first notes in 1835. It issued Consolidated Banknotes in 1929, as well as its own Northern Ireland issue.

In 1966 the Irish Business of the Bank was taken over by a new company called The National Bank of Ireland Ltd., which was set up as a subsidiary of The Bank of Ireland Group. The National Bank was subsequently taken over by the Bank of Ireland.

The Northern Bank Ltd 1824

Established as The Northern Banking Company on 1 August 1824, with 264 shareholders, it took over the business of Montgomery's Private Bank, operating since 1809. The Northern Bank opened on 1 January 1825 in Belfast and commenced the issue of banknotes. Northern notes were always printed on both sides.

In 1867 the Bank was incorporated. It changed its name to The Northern Banking Company Ltd. on 1 September 1883. In 1888 the Bank bought the business of Ball & Co., Dublin, for £22,500, and opened an office there.

On 1 January 1929 the bank changed its name to The Northern Bank Ltd. It issued Consolidated Banknotes in 1929, as well as its own Northern Ireland issue. It continues to issue banknotes in Northern Ireland to this day.

The Northern Bank was taken over by The Midland Bank Group in 1965 and had the Belfast bank merged into it in 1970. In 1987 Midland sold the Northern Bank to National Australia Bank. After this takeover, the identity of the former Northern Bank in the Republic of Ireland was changed in name to National Irish Bank, with the Northern Bank identity remaining only in Northern Ireland.

The Provident Bank of Ireland 1837–1840

This bank was founded in Dublin by Thomas Mooney, founder of the former Agricultural & Commercial. Despite being in Dublin, the bank was able to issue banknotes as it had fewer than 6 shareholders. It was constituted in such a way that it could draw on funds from outside of its shareholder base.

The bank was intended as a farmers' bank and only ever had one office. It failed to raise sufficient capital for its activities and ceased operations in December 1839, with its owners being adjudicated bankrupt on 14 October 1840. It appears that the vast bulk of its banknotes were paid off by April 1841.

The Provincial Bank of Ireland Ltd. 1825

Founded by Thomas Joplin and others in London in 1825 with 689 shareholders, the Provincial Bank of Ireland opened its first branch in Cork on 1 September 1825. Its primary aim was to introduce English capital into Ireland outside of the Dublin area. It was organised along the lines of the Scottish banks of the day, and imported Scottish expertise. The Provincial bank initially employed La Touche, a private bank, as its agency in Dublin. It opened an office at 60 South William St., Dublin in 1836 where it redeemed its banknotes, but did not issue or re-issue them, in accordance with the law.

The Provincial Bank commenced its initial note issue in 1825. It issued Consolidated Banknotes in 1929, as well as its own Northern Ireland issue.

In 1966 The Provincial Bank of Ireland merged with The Munster & Leinster Bank and The Royal Bank of Ireland to form Allied Irish Banks. The new bank group retained the Provincial Bank identity in Northern Ireland and continued to issue banknotes there as the Provincial Bank of Ireland until 1981 when it issued banknotes under the title of Allied Irish Banks. It changed its title to First Trust Bank in 1994, and still continues to issue its own notes under that title.

The Royal Bank of Ireland 1836–1966

The Royal Bank was founded on 1 September 1836 with 309 shareholders and commenced business in Dublin on 26 September. It took over the operations of private bankers Sir Robert Shaw, Bart & Co. which had been in existence since 1799 as Leighton, Needham & Shaw, based in Foster Place, Dublin, where the Royal established its office.

At one point, a sizeable number of Royal Bank shares were held by the Directors of The Agricultural & Commercial Bank with a view to merging the two banks, but the Agricultural & Commercial failed prior to the completion of negotiations.

The Royal Bank of Ireland sought the right to register as a bank of note issue in 1844, without success, and was precluded from doing so thereafter by the 1845 Act. It remained a Dublin bank until the 1860s, when it began to open branches further afield. In 1923, it bought the 20 branches of the Belfast Banking Company which were located in the Irish Free State. The Royal Bank finally got the right to issue its own banknotes in 1929, as part of the Consolidated Banknote issue.

The Bank merged with The Munster & Leinster Bank and The Provincial Bank of Ireland in 1966 to form Allied Irish Banks.

The Southern Bank of Ireland 1837

Founded in Cork in March 1837 by some former officials of the Agricultural & Commercial. The Southern Bank lasted less than a year, and appears to have operated on the fringe of legality. It issued one series of banknotes, but had little in the way of funds to back them.

The Ulster Bank Ltd 1836

The Ulster Banking Company was founded on 22 February 1836 as a result of a meeting in Belfast to open a National Bank branch. The bank was established on 1 April 1836 with approximately 830 shareholders. It was to have started business on 1 June 1836, which is the date on its first banknotes. Final arrangements had not been completed, however, and the bank did not start to operate until 1 July 1836. The Ulster Banking Co. opened an office in Dublin in 1862, and changed its name to The Ulster Bank Ltd. on 1 September 1883. In 1917 the bank's share capital was bought up by the London County & Westminster Bank Ltd. The Ulster Bank remains part of The National Westminster Bank Group, but retains its Ulster Bank identity in Ireland.

It issued the full range of Consolidated Banknotes in 1929, as well as its own Northern Ireland issue. The bank continues to issue banknotes in Northern Ireland.

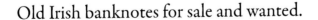

Irish Government Banknotes 1928 – 2001

Currency Commission Ireland 1928–1942
Central Bank of Ireland 1943–2001

Section 1	Consolidated Bank Notes	1929–1941	21
Section 2	Legal Tender A Series Notes	1928–1977	37
Section 3	Legal Tender B Series Notes	1976–1993	57
Section 4	Legal Tender C Series Notes	1992–2001	63

The following symbols are used

< "Less than"	~ "Approximately"
> "Greater than"	≤ "Less than or equal to"
<< "Much less than"	≥ "Greater than or equal to"
>> "Much greater than"	

Indications of relative rarity – One to Six stars. Latest revision, 2014.
In an effort to roughly indicate relative rarity all known scarcer notes are listed and marked according to their degree of rarity. Where an entire Type of any Series is at least of a particular degree of rarity, this is indicated with stars before the general Identification E number of that Type. For example all Type 6 £50 notes are at least ** rare. This is indicated at the beginning of the entry for these notes. Where notes are rarer than the general rarity of a Type, this is indicated separately before each date or year. Degrees of rarity are adjusted from time to time to reflect new finds. A good example of such an adjustment is in the case of E-010, Hibernian Bank Hodges signature £1 note for which many more examples have surfaced since 1999. Consequently, it has fewer stars now than it did then.

*	Uncommon.	****	Very rare.
**	Scarce.	*****	Extremely rare.
***	Rare.	******	Only one or two examples may exist.

Section 1

Irish Government Banknotes
Currency Commission Ireland
Consolidated Banknotes
1929 – 1941

PRE-PRODUCTION
SPECIMEN AND TRIAL PRINTINGS

Prior to the production of the Consolidated Banknotes trial printings were produced in various colours of each denomination. These Specimens were printed on various substrates, some uniface on card and paper and some double sided. They carried no bank title.

BRANCHLESS TRIALS
Various denominations seen printed on card and on paper.

TS–001   **10/- notes – Type 1S.**
Print:

	€			
VG	Fine	VF	EF	UNC
350	620	1000	1650	2000

TS–002   **£1 notes – Type 1S.**
Print:

	€			
VG	Fine	VF	EF	UNC
250	320	400	550	600

TS–003   **£5 notes – Type 1S.**
Print:

	€			
VG	Fine	VF	EF	UNC
350	550	700	900	1000

TS–004   **£10 notes – Type 1S.**
Print:

	€			
VG	Fine	VF	EF	UNC
350	620	1000	1200	1300

TS–005   **£20 notes – Type 1S.**
Print:

	€			
VG	Fine	VF	EF	UNC
850	1300	1400	1650	2000

TS–006   **£50 notes – Type 1S.**
Print:

	€			
VG	Fine	VF	EF	UNC
850	1300	1400	1650	2000

TS–007   **£100 notes – Type 1S.**
Print:

	€			
VG	Fine	VF	EF	UNC
850	1300	1400	1650	2000

THE BANK OF IRELAND
Two Types 1929 – 1940

E–001 **£1 notes – Type 1B. [1929 – 1938] J. A. Gargan** €

		Poor	VG	Fine	VF	EF	UNC
Print: ~ 9,000,000
14 Dates. 6.5.29 – 4.10.38 · · · 80 · 200 · 300 · 400 · 600 · 800
1 Variety: 26.7.33 small prefix digits.

001SC. **5.9.78** SPECIMEN — *1000*
001SX. **5.9.78** SPECIMEN TDLR in non-standard colours — *1000*

E–002 **£1 notes – Type 2B. [1939 – 1940] H. J. Johnston** €

Print: ≥ 400,000 · · · Poor VG Fine VF EF UNC
4 Dates. 10.1.39 – 2.1.40 · · · 80 200 300 400 600 800
+2.1.40 · · · Probably never issued

*E–003 **£5 notes – Type 1B. [1929 – 1931] J. A. Gargan** €

Print: ~ 200,000 · · · Poor VG Fine VF EF UNC
3 Dates. 6.5.29 – 8.5.31 · · · 150 350 550 1100 1000 2500
003SC. **5.9.78** SPECIMEN — *1500*
003SX. **5.9.78** SPECIMEN TDLR in non-standard colours *1000* *1500*

*E–004 **£5 notes – Type 2B. [1939] H. J. Johnston** €

Print: ~ 100,000 · · · Poor VG Fine VF EF UNC
1 Date. 14.9.39 · · · 150 350 550 1500 1800 2500

E–005 **£10 notes – Type 1B. [1929] J. A. Gargan €

Print: 26,000 (9,050 not issued) · · · Poor VG Fine VF EF UNC
1 Date. 6.5.29 · · · 400 900 1800 2800 4000 5000
005SC. **5.9.78** SPECIMEN — *2500*
005SX. **5.9.78** SPECIMEN TDLR in non-standard colours *1500* *2500*

E–006 **£20 notes – Type 1B. [1929] J. A. Gargan** €

Print: · · · Poor VG Fine VF EF UNC
1 Date. 6.5.29 · · · No notes outstanding
006SC. **5.9.78** SPECIMEN — *4000*
006SX. **5.9.78** SPECIMEN TDLR in non-standard colours *2500* *4000*

E–007 **£50 notes – Type 1B. [1929] J. A. Gargan** €

Print: · · · Poor VG Fine VF EF UNC
1 Date. 6.5.29 · · · No notes outstanding
007SC. **5.9.78** SPECIMEN — *4500*
007SX. **5.9.78** SPECIMEN TDLR in non-standard colours *2500* *4500*

E–008 **£100 notes – Type 1B. [1929] J. A. Gargan** €

Print: · · · Poor VG Fine VF EF UNC
1 Date. 6.5.29 · · · No notes outstanding
008SC. **5.9.78** SPECIMEN — *4500*
008SX. **5.9.78** SPECIMEN TDLR in non-standard colours *2500* *4500*

+ SX Specimens exist both with and without De La Rue overprints.

THE HIBERNIAN BANK LTD
Two Types 1929 – 1940

*E–009   **£1 notes – Type 1H. [1929 – 1938] H. J. Campbell** €

Print: ~ 2,300,000
16 Dates. 6.5.29 – 4.5.39
***7.1.31
1 Variety: **26.7.33 small prefix digits.

Poor	VG	Fine	VF	EF	UNC
80	250	350	600	1000	1400

*E–010   **£1 notes – Type 2H. [1939 – 1940] A. K. Hodges** €

Print: ~ 200,000
2 Dates. 5.8.39 – 9.2.40
+9.2.40

Poor	VG	Fine	VF	EF	UNC
80	250	350	600	1000	1400
				Probably never issued	

*E–011   **£5 notes – Type 1H. [1929 – 1938] H. J. Campbell** €

Print: ~ 220,000
7 Dates. 6.5.29 – 8.5.39
***29.1.31

Poor	VG	Fine	VF	EF	UNC
150	350	700	1300	2500	4000

E–012   **£5 notes – Type 2H. [1939] A. K. Hodges** €

Print:
1 Date. 13.9.39

Poor	VG	Fine	VF	EF	UNC
			Probably never issued		

E–013   **£10 notes – Type 1H. [1929 – 1931] H. J. Campbell €

Print: ~ 35,000
3 Dates. 6.5.29 – 5.12.31

Poor	VG	Fine	VF	EF	UNC
550	1400	2200	4000	5500	8000

E–014   **£10 notes – Type 2H. [1939] A. K. Hodges** €

Print:
1 Date. 24.7.39

Poor	VG	Fine	VF	EF	UNC
			Probably never issued		

E–015   **£20 notes: Type 1H. [1929] H. J. Campbell** €

Print:
1 Date. 6.5.29

Poor	VG	Fine	VF	EF	UNC
			No notes outstanding		

THE MUNSTER AND LEINSTER BANK LTD
Two Types 1929 – 1940

E–016 **£1 notes – Type 1M. [1929 – 1935] J. L. Gubbins** €

Print: ~ 2,500,000

	Poor	VG	Fine	VF	EF	UNC
7 Dates. 6.5.29 – 5.3.35	80	200	300	400	600	800

1 Variety: 26.7.33 small prefix digits.

E–017 **£1 notes – Type 2M. [1936 – 1940] A. E. Hosford** €

Print: ~ 2,500,000

	Poor	VG	Fine	VF	EF	UNC
10 Dates. 7.2.36 – 6.2.40	80	200	300	400	600	800
***6.2.40	Probably never issued					2000

Several UNC examples of £1, 6.2.40 exist in the archives of The Central Bank of Ireland.

*E–018 **£5 notes – Type 1M. [1929 – 1933] J. L. Gubbins** €

Print: ≥ 110,000

	Poor	VG	Fine	VF	EF	UNC
4 Dates. 6.5.29 – 5.3.33	150	400	550	1200	1600	2800

***29.1.31

*E–019 **£5 notes – Type 2M. [1938 – 1939] A. E. Hosford** €

Print: ~ 65,000

	Poor	VG	Fine	VF	EF	UNC
4 Dates. 7.4.38 – 22.9.39	150	400	650	1300	1700	2800

*E–020 **£10 notes – Type 1M. [1929 – 1931] J. L. Gubbins** €

Print: ≥ 60,000

	Poor	VG	Fine	VF	EF	UNC
3 Dates. 6.5.29 – 5.12.31	400	1000	1800	2800	4000	5000

*E–021 **£10 notes – Type 2M. [1938 – 1939] A. E. Hosford** €

Print: ~ 20,000

	Poor	VG	Fine	VF	EF	UNC
2 Dates. 7.3.38 – 4.8.39	400	1000	1800	2800	4000	5000

E–022 **£20 notes – Type 1M. [1929] J. L. Gubbins** €

Print: ~

	Poor	VG	Fine	VF	EF	UNC
1 Date. 6.5.29	No notes outstanding					

E–023 **£50 notes – Type 1M. [1929] J. L. Gubbins** €

Print: ~

	Poor	VG	Fine	VF	EF	UNC
1 Date. 6.5.29	No notes outstanding					

E–024 **£100 notes – Type 1M. [1929] J. L. Gubbins** €

Print: ~

	Poor	VG	Fine	VF	EF	UNC
1 Date. 6.5.29	No notes outstanding					

+   Images of £20, £50 and £100 notes of the the Munster & Leinster Bank exist and have become available for illustration, courtesy of The Central Bank of Ireland.
There are no banknotes of these denominations outstanding from any bank. None will ever be available to collectors. Therefore, despite the existence of these denominations, no valuations are given for the notes as they are not available to collectors. These images are of academic interest only.

THE NATIONAL BANK LTD
One Type 1929 – 1940

E–025 **£1 notes – Type 1N. [1929 – 1940] H. A. Russell** €

Print: ~ 5,000,000
17 Dates. 6.5.29 – 4.1.40
1 Variety: 26.7.33 small prefix digits.
+4.1.40

Poor	VG	Fine	VF	EF	UNC
80	200	300	400	600	800

Probably never issued

E–026 **£5 notes – Type 1N. [1929 – 1939] H. A. Russell** €

Print: ~ 450,000
8 Dates. 6.5.29 – 16.9.39
***29.1.31

Poor	VG	Fine	VF	EF	UNC
150	450	600	1100	1600	2500

*E–027 **£10 notes – Type 1N. [1929 – 1939] H. A. Russell** €

Print: ≥ 52,000
4 Dates. 6.5.29 – 31.7.39

Poor	VG	Fine	VF	EF	UNC
400	1000	1800	2800	4000	5000

Six Northern Bank £10 notes are known to exist.

+   There exists a run of over seventy National Bank £5 notes dated 15.3.33 in gEF-AU grade.

THE NORTHERN BANK LTD
Four Types 1929 – 1940

E–028
****
£1 notes – Type 1E. [1929] S. W. Knox

Print:

2 Dates. 6.5.29 – 10.6.29

€

Poor	VG	Fine	VF	EF	UNC
700	2000	3000	5000	6000	–

**E–029
£1 notes – Type 2E. [1931] H. H. Stewart

Print: ~ 200,000

1 Date. 7.1.31

€

Poor	VG	Fine	VF	EF	UNC
300	1000	1900	3500	5000	6000

+E–030
£1 notes – Type 4E. [1939 – 1940] A. P. Tibbey

Print: 75,000

+2 Dates. 9.10.39 – 8.1.40

€

Poor	VG	Fine	VF	EF	UNC
			Probably never issued		

***E–031
£5 notes – Type 1E. [1929] S. W. Knox

Print: 28,000

1 Date. 6.5.29

€

Poor	VG	Fine	VF	EF	UNC
700	3500	5500	7500	8500	–

**E–032
£5 notes – Type 2E. [1931 – 1933] H. H. Stewart

Print: ≥ 55,000

3 Dates. 29.1.31 – 15.3.33

€

Poor	VG	Fine	VF	EF	UNC
350	2500	3500	5000	6000	–

+E–033
£5 notes – Type 3E. [1939] W. F. Scott

Print:

+1 Date. 15.9.39

€

Poor	VG	Fine	VF	EF	UNC
			Probably never issued		

E–034
*****
£10 notes – Type 1E. [1929] S. W. Knox

Print: 13,000

1 Date. 6.5.29

€

Poor	VG	Fine	VF	EF	UNC
2000	10000	18000	–	–	–

E–035
£20 notes – Type 1E. [1929] S. W. Knox

Print: 3,000

1 Date. 6.5.29

€

Poor	VG	Fine	VF	EF	UNC
			No notes outstanding		

+   Type 3E £5 notes and Type 4E £1 notes never entered circulation.

THE PROVINCIAL BANK OF IRELAND LTD
Three Types 1929 – 1940

*E–036 **£1 notes – Type 1P. [1929] Hume Robertson** €

Print: ~ 600,000

2 Dates. 6.5.29 – 10.6.29

Poor	VG	Fine	VF	EF	UNC
80	350	600	900	1100	1300

E–037 **£1 notes – Type 2P. [1931 – 1936] F. S. Forde** €

Print: ≤ 700,000

5 Dates. 7.1.31 – 5.9.36

Poor	VG	Fine	VF	EF	UNC
80	250	300	500	700	1200

E–038 **£1 notes – Type 3. [1937 – 1940] G. A. Kennedy** €

Print: ~ 1,000,000

8 Dates. 3.6.37 – 19.1.40

+19.1.40

Poor	VG	Fine	VF	EF	UNC
80	250	300	500	700	1200
					Probably never issued

E–039 **£5 notes – Type 1P. [1929] Hume Robertson €

Print: ≥ 35,000

1 Date. 6.5.29

Poor	VG	Fine	VF	EF	UNC
150	700	1000	2500	3000	3500

E–040 **£5 notes – Type 2P. [1931] F. S. Forde** €

Print: ~ 95,000

2 Dates. 29.1.31 – 8.5.31

Poor	VG	Fine	VF	EF	UNC
150	450	600	1100	1800	3000

E–041 **£5 notes – Type 3P. [1939] G. A. Kennedy €

Print: ≥ 10,000

2 Dates. 3.4.39 – 19.9.39

Poor	VG	Fine	VF	EF	UNC
150	700	1000	1800	2400	3000

E–042 **£10 notes – Type 1P. [1929] Hume Robertson €

Print: ~ 20,000

1 Date. 6.5.29

Poor	VG	Fine	VF	EF	UNC
350	1100	2500	4000	6500	8000

*E–043 **£10 notes – Type 2P. [1931] F. S. Forde** €

Print: ~ 13,000

1 Date. 2.10.31

Poor	VG	Fine	VF	EF	UNC
250	900	1800	2800	4000	6000

***E–044 **£10 notes – Type 3P. [1939] G. A. Kennedy** €

Print:

1 Date. 17.7.39

Poor	VG	Fine	VF	EF	UNC
900	3000	4000	6000	8000	10000

E–045 **£20 notes – Type 1P. [1929] Hume Robertson** €

Print:

1 Date. 6.5.29

Poor	VG	Fine	VF	EF	UNC
					No notes outstanding

THE ROYAL BANK OF IRELAND LTD
Three Types 1929 – 1941

E–046 **£1 notes – Type 1R. [1929 – 1931] G. A. Stanley €

Print: ~ 800,000

	Poor	VG	Fine	VF	EF	UNC
3 Dates. 6.5.29 – 7.1.31	150	350	600	750	1500	1600

*E–047 **£1 notes – Type 2R. [1931 – 1939] David R. Mack** €

Print: ~ 1,700,000

	Poor	VG	Fine	VF	EF	UNC
11 Dates. 8.12.31 – 8.3.39	130	280	450	600	1200	1500

1 Variety: 26.7.33 small prefix digits.

**2.4.36

*E–048 **£1 notes – Type 3R. [1939 – 1941] J. S. Wilson** €

Print: > 200,000

	Poor	VG	Fine	VF	EF	UNC
5 Dates. 2.5.39 – 30.4.41	150	280	450	600	1200	1500
+5.2.40, 30.4.41				Probably never issued		

E–049 **£5 notes – Type 1R. [1929] G. A. Stanley €

Print: ~ 35,000

	Poor	VG	Fine	VF	EF	UNC
1 Date. 6.5.29	350	1300	1800	3500	6000	7000

E–050 **£5 notes – Type 2R. [1931] David R. Mack €

Print: > 15,000

	Poor	VG	Fine	VF	EF	UNC
2 Dates. 29.1.31 – 8.5.31	350	1100	1600	3500	6000	7000

+E–051 **£5 notes – Type 3R. [1939] J. S. Wilson** €

Print:

	Poor	VG	Fine	VF	EF	UNC
1 Date. 21.1.39				Probably never issued		

***E–052 **£10 notes – Type 1R. [1929] G. A. Stanley** €

Print: ~ 15,000

	Poor	VG	Fine	VF	EF	UNC
1 Date. 6.5.29	900	2200	4000	7000	13000	15000

E–053 **£20 notes – Type 1R. [1929] G. A. Stanley** €

Print:

	Poor	VG	Fine	VF	EF	UNC
1 Date. 6.5.29				No notes outstanding		

E–054 **£50 notes – Type 1R. [1929] G. A. Stanley** €

Print:

	Poor	VG	Fine	VF	EF	UNC
1 Date. 6.5.29				No notes outstanding		

E–055 **£100 notes – Type 1R. [1929] G. A. Stanley** €

Print:

	Poor	VG	Fine	VF	EF	UNC
1 Date. 6.5.29				No notes outstanding		

THE ULSTER BANK LTD
Two Types 1929 – 1940

E–056 **£1 notes – Type 1U. [1929 – 1935] C. W. Patton

Print: ~ 700,000

8 Dates. 6.5.29 – 17.6.35

1 Variety: 26.7.33 small prefix digits.

	Poor	VG	Fine	VF	EF	UNC
€	150	550	750	1200	1600	1800

E–057 **£1 notes – Type 2U. [1936 – 1940] C. W. Lester

Print: ~ 500,000

7 Dates. 3.11.36 – 7.2.40

+7.2.40

	Poor	VG	Fine	VF	EF	UNC
€	130	550	750	1200	1600	1800

Probably never issued

E–058 **£5 notes – Type 1U. [1929 – 1933] C. W. Patton

Print: ~ 85,000

4 Dates. 6.5.29 – 15.3.33

	Poor	VG	Fine	VF	EF	UNC
€	250	950	1800	2500	4000	5000

E–059 **£5 notes – Type 2U. [1938 – 1939] C. W. Lester

Print: ~ 85,000

3 Dates. 3.5.38 – 11.9.39

	Poor	VG	Fine	VF	EF	UNC
€	250	950	1800	2500	4000	5000

***E–060 **£10 notes – Type 1U. [1929] C. W. Patton**

Print: ~ 10,000

1 Date. 6.5.29

	Poor	VG	Fine	VF	EF	UNC
€	800	2200	4000	7000	10000	15000

***E–061 **£10 notes – Type 2U. [1938 – 1939] C. W. Lester**

Print: > 5,000

2 Dates. 4.2.38 – 9.8.39

	Poor	VG	Fine	VF	EF	UNC
€	800	2200	4000	7000	10000	15000

E–062 **£20 notes – Type 1U. [1929] C. W. Patton**

Print:

1 Date. 6.5.29

	Poor	VG	Fine	VF	EF	UNC
€			No notes outstanding			

E–063 **£50 notes – Type 1U. [1929] C. W. Patton**

Print:

1 Date. 6.5.29

	Poor	VG	Fine	VF	EF	UNC
€			No notes outstanding			

E–064 **£100 notes – Type 1U. [1929] C. W. Patton**

Print:

1 Date. 6.5.29

	Poor	VG	Fine	VF	EF	UNC
€			No notes outstanding			

Section 2

Irish Government Banknotes

Currency Commission Ireland & Central Bank of Ireland

Legal Tender A Series Banknotes
1928 – 1977

Ten Shilling Nótes
1928 – 1968

**E–065 TYPE 1. [1928]

CURRENCY COMMISSION IRISH FREE STATE – Fractional prefix
Joseph Brennan, J. J. McElligott.

	Poor	VG	Fine	VF	EF	UNC
Print: ~ 4,000,000						
2 Dates. 10.9.28	100	350	700	1100	1500	2500
23.10.28	100	350	500	900	1500	2000
065SC. 13.5.06 SPECIMEN					650	1000

*E–066 TYPE 2. [1929 – 1937]

CURRENCY COMMISSION IRISH FREE STATE – Linear prefix
Joseph Brennan, J. J. McElligott.

	Poor	VG	Fine	VF	EF	UNC
Print: ≤ 30,000,000						
42 Dates. 31.12.29 – 4.8.37		120	260	400	700	1000
**31.12.29	100	250	500	1300	1800	2500

E–067 TYPE 3. [1938 – 1939]

CURRENCY COMMISSION IRELAND
Joseph Brennan, J. J. McElligott. "Rúnaidhe na Roinne Airgeadais"

	VG	Fine	VF	EF	UNC
Print: ≥ 14,800,000					
30 Dates. 17.1.38 – 20.12.39	40	100	250	300	450
067SC. 13.5.06 SPECIMEN					800

E–068 TYPE 4. [1940 – 1941]

CURRENCY COMMISSION IRELAND – Emergency Tracer Overprint Code
Joseph Brennan, J. J. McElligott.
ETO CODES: Blue Ⓗ Green Ⓚ Brown Ⓙ

	VG	Fine	VF	EF	UNC
Print: ≥ 12,100,000					
27 Dates.	65	100	160	200	350
13 dates Ⓗ 30.7.40 – 9.10.40					
6 dates Ⓚ 7.11.40 – 9.4.41					
7 dates Ⓙ 23.5.41 – 1.12.41					
****1.12.41 Ⓙ					
Varieties: *****1.12.41 Ⓚ End Displaced Code	400	1000			

E–069   TYPE 5. [1943 – 1944]

CENTRAL BANK OF IRELAND – Emergency Tracer Overprint Code
Joseph Brennan, J. J. McElligott.
ETO CODES: orange Ⓛ   grey Ⓜ   black Ⓡ   purple Ⓔ   €

Print: ≥ 11,700,000	VG	Fine	VF	EF	UNC
26 Dates.	65	100	160	200	350
*** 10.8.43, 4.9.43	100	140	250	350	450
6 dates Ⓛ 6.2.43 – 10.4.43					
7 dates Ⓜ 8.5.43 – 10.8.43					
7 dates Ⓡ 4.9.43 – 3.12.43					
6 dates Ⓔ 17.12.43 – 28.3.44					
Varieties: *****10.8.43 Ⓛ Middle Displaced Code	400	1000			
*****28.3.44 Ⓡ End Displaced Code	400	1000			
069SC. 13.5.06 Ⓛ SPECIMEN					*1000*

E–070   TYPE 6. [1945 – 1950]

CENTRAL BANK OF IRELAND – ETO Code discontinued
Joseph Brennan, J. J. McElligott.   €

Print: ~ 42,000,000	VG	Fine	VF	EF	UNC
92 Dates. 15.5.45 – 3.10.50	10	25	45	60	130
***12.12.45, 13.8.46, 14.7.47, 17.6.49, 24.1.50	100	150	170		
*10.2.49					
070SC. 13.5.06 SPECIMEN					*560*

E–071   TYPE 7. [1951 – 1952]

CENTRAL BANK OF IRELAND – Serial Numbers extended
Joseph Brennan, J. J. McElligott.   €

Print: ~ 40,000,000	VG	Fine	VF	EF	UNC
2 Dates. 12.9.51 – 22.10.52	5	10	18	30	70

*E–072   TYPE 8. [1955]

CENTRAL BANK OF IRELAND – Signature variation
J. J. McElligott, O. J. Redmond. "Rúnaí na Roinne Airgeadais"   €

Print: ~ 6,000,000	VG	Fine	VF	EF	UNC
1 Date. 19.10.55	5	10	60	170	280
072SC. 13.5.06 SPECIMEN					*500*

E–073   TYPE 9. [1957 – 1959]

CENTRAL BANK OF IRELAND – Signature variation
J. J. McElligott, T. K. Whitaker.   €

Print: ~ 42,000,000	VG	Fine	VF	EF	UNC
3 Dates. 28.5.57 – 1.9.59	5	10	18	30	70
*11.3.59 ~ 2,500,000				50	120

E–074   TYPE 11. [1962 – 1968]

CENTRAL BANK OF IRELAND – Signature variation
"STERLING" promise dropped
M. Ó Muimhneacháin, T. K. Whitaker.   €

Print: 100,000,000	VG	Fine	VF	EF	UNC
6 Dates. 3.1.62 – 6.6.68	3	8	18	25	35
1962-1966	3	8	18	25	50
Varieties: 25.5.66, 6.6.68 Small date typeface.					
074SC. 2.3.02 SPECIMEN					*500*
074SP. various dates SPECIMEN					*300*

One Pound Notes
1928 – 1976

*E–075 **TYPE 1. [1928]**
CURRENCY COMMISSION IRISH FREE STATE – Fractional prefix
Joseph Brennan, J. J. McElligott.

€

Print: ~ 6,000,000	Poor	VG	Fine	VF	EF	UNC
2 Dates. 10.9.28	30	150	250	450	1500	2000
23.10.28	20	100	200	350	1000	1500
075SC. 13.5.06 SPECIMEN						*560*

E–076 **TYPE 2. [1930 – 1937]**
CURRENCY COMMISSION IRISH FREE STATE – Linear prefix
Joseph Brennan, J. J. McElligott.

€

Print: ≥ 22,500,000	VG	Fine	VF	EF	UNC
36 Dates. 4.7.30 – 23.12.37	20	70	200	500	1100
*2.1.36, **7.1.37	50	150	250	600	1100

E–077 **TYPE 3. [1939]**
CURRENCY COMMISSION IRELAND
Joseph Brennan, J. J. McElligott. "Rúnaidhe na Roinne Airgeadais"   €

Print: ~ 6,000,000	VG	Fine	VF	EF	UNC
12 Dates. 9.1.39 – 8.12.39	20	60	160	250	400

E–078 **TYPE 4. [1941 – 1942]**
CURRENCY COMMISSION IRELAND – Emergency Tracer Overprint Code
Joseph Brennan, J. J. McElligott.
ETO CODES: purple Ⓣ red Ⓑ brown Ⓟ grey-green Ⓥ   €

Print: ~ 12,100,000	VG	Fine	VF	EF	UNC
25 Dates.	30	70	180	250	400
6 dates Ⓣ 14.3.41 – 10.5.41					
7 dates Ⓑ 5.6.41 – 3.9.41					
6 dates Ⓟ 3.10.41 – 5.3.42					
6 dates Ⓥ 1.4.42 – 22.9.42					
***3.9.41	100	140	250	270	400
Varieties: *****3.9.41 Ⓣ Middle Displaced Code	400	1000			
*****22.9.42 Ⓟ End Displaced Code	400	1000			

E–079 **TYPE 5. [1943–1944]**
CENTRAL BANK OF IRELAND – Emergency Tracer Overprint Code
Joseph Brennan, J. J. McElligott.
ETO CODES: black Ⓖ   blue Ⓨ   red Ⓔ   pink Ⓕ

	VG	Fine	VF	EF	UNC
Print: ≥ 12,100,000					€
26 Dates.	30	70	180	250	400
6 dates Ⓖ 3.2.43 – 2.7.43					
7 dates Ⓨ 5.7.43 – 29.10.43					
6 dates Ⓔ 3.6.44 – 1.9.44					
6 dates Ⓕ 15.9.44 – 6.12.44					
** 29.10.43, 3.6.44	100	140	250	270	300
Varieties: *****29.10.43 Ⓡ Middle Displaced Code	400	1000			
*****6.12.44 Ⓔ End Displaced Code	400	1000			
079SC. 13.5.06 Ⓖ SPECIMEN					1000

E–080 **TYPE 6. [1945 – 1950]**
CENTRAL BANK OF IRELAND – ETO Code discontinued
Joseph Brennan, J. J. McElligott.

	VG	Fine	VF	EF	UNC
Print: ~ 62,000,000					€
131 Dates.12.4.45 – 11.12.50	5	15	25	50	90
***12.4.45, 5.8.49, 18.4.50, 6.6.50, 11.12.50	10	25	55	90	130
*16.5.45, 20.11.50, 28.11.50, 2.12.50, 4.12.50	-	15	30	70	110
Variations: Non-sequential dating.					
080SC. 13.5.06 SPECIMEN					560

E–081 **TYPE 7. [1951 – 1952]**
CENTRAL BANK OF IRELAND – Serial numbers extended
Joseph Brennan, J. J. McElligott.

	VG	Fine	VF	EF	UNC
Print: ~ 45,000,000					€
2 Dates. 11.9.51 – 26.8.52	-	-	10	25	50

E–082 **TYPE 8. [1954 – 1955]**
CENTRAL BANK OF IRELAND – Signature variation
J. J. McElligott, O. J. Redmond. "Rúnaí na Roinne Airgeadais"

	VG	Fine	VF	EF	UNC
Print: ~ 21,000,000					€
2 Dates. 6.1.54 – 25.10.55	-	-	10	25	50
122SC. 13.5.06 SPECIMEN					560

NOTE: The illustrated £1 note, 12.4.45 94N 026041 was for more than 25 years the only Legal Tender £1 note date for which an example had not been recorded. This one finally turned up in 2009.

E–083   TYPE 9. [1957 – 1960]

CENTRAL BANK OF IRELAND – Signature variation
J. J. McElligott, T. K. Whitaker.

Print: ~ 70,000,000		VG	Fine	€ VF	EF	UNC
4 Dates. 12.6.57 – 18.5.60		-	-	8	13	40
Varieties:	31.12.58 Dark green blank.	-	-	8	13	40
	2.9.59, 18.5.60 Design II.	-	-	8	13	40
Variations:	2.9.59, 18.5.60 **Mulberry.	-	4	15	25	80
083SC. 31.12.99 SPECIMEN						500
083SP. 13.5.06 SPECIMEN						350

E–084   TYPE 11. [1962 – 1968]

CENTRAL BANK OF IRELAND – Signature variation
"STERLING" promise dropped
M. Ó Muimhneacháin, T. K. Whitaker.

Print: ~ 163,000,000		VG	Fine	€ VF	EF	UNC
8 Dates. 16.3.62 – 8.10.68		-	-	8	13	30
***3.4.63 F prefix		-	8	20	30	60
Varieties:	11.3.63 Experimental note. Issued May 1974.	-	4	8	13	30
Variations:	16.3.62, 11.3.63, 3.4.63 **Mulberry.		4	8	13	50
084SC. 13.5.06 SPECIMEN						560
084SP. various issued note dates SPECIMEN						200

E–085   TYPE 12. [1969 – 1970]

CENTRAL BANK OF IRELAND – Signature variation
T. K. Whitaker, C. H. Murray.

Print: ~ 51,000,000		VG	Fine	€ VF	EF	UNC
4 Dates. 1.3.69 – 17.9.70		-	-	8	13	30
Varieties:	1.3.69, 23.5.69 Small date typeface.	-	-	8	13	30

E–086   TYPE 13. [1971 – 1975]

CENTRAL BANK OF IRELAND – Metallic security thread introduced
T. K. Whitaker, C. H. Murray.

Print: 200,000,000		VG	Fine	€ VF	EF	UNC
4 Dates. 8.7.71 – 21.4.75		-	-	-	8	20
** 28.6.72 K prefix		-	-	-	8	60
2 Replacements. *17.5.74 S, *21.4.75 00A		-	5	15	30	60
Varieties:	17.5.74, 21.4.75 Sans-serif typeface.	-	-	-	8	20
086SC. 00.1.00 SPECIMEN, sans-serif						560

E–087   TYPE 14. [1976]

CENTRAL BANK OF IRELAND – Signature variation
C. H. Murray, M. O Murchú.

Print: ~ 54,000,000	VG	Fine	€ VF	EF	UNC
1 Date. 30.9.76	-	-	-	8	20
Replacement. *00A	-	5	15	30	60

A full list of all observed replacement note dates along with known serial number brackets may be viewed on *http://www.irishpapermoney.com/replacements/star0.html*

Five Pound Notes
1928 – 1975

*E–088   **TYPE 1. [1928]**
CURRENCY COMMISSION IRISH FREE STATE – Fractional prefix
Joseph Brennan, J J McElligott.

Print: ~ 1,300,000	Poor	VG	Fine	VF	EF	UNC
2 Dates. **10.9.28	60	280	600	1300	1800	2800
*23.10.28	40	180	400	700	1600	1800
088SC. 13.5.06 SPECIMEN						*700*

*E–089   **TYPE 2. [1932 – 1937]**
CURRENCY COMMISSION IRISH FREE STATE – Linear prefix
Joseph Brennan, J. J. McElligott.

Print: ~ 1,630,000	VG	Fine	VF	EF	UNC
18 Dates. 7.6.32 – 19.8.37	80	180	350	1000	1300
**6.4.37, 19.8.37	100	200	400	1000	1300
***4.2.33	250	400	600		

E–090   **TYPE 3. [1938 – 1939]**
CURRENCY COMMISSION IRELAND
Joseph Brennan, J J McElliogtt. "Rúnaidhe na Roinne Airgeadais"

Print: ~ 1,200,000	VG	Fine	VF	EF	UNC
15 Dates. 5.7.38 – 1.11.39	30	80	180	350	600
**1.11.39	30	80	200	400	

E–091   **TYPE 4. [1940 – 1942]**
CURRENCY COMMISSION IRELAND – Emergency Tracer Overprint Code
Joseph Brennan, J. J. McElligott.
ETO CODES: green Ⓐ purple Ⓒ blue Ⓓ

Print: ~ 1,970,000	VG	Fine	VF	EF	UNC
23 Dates.	30	150	250	400	600
7 dates Ⓐ 12.9.40 – 16.10.40					
8 dates Ⓒ 2.5.41 – 3.12.41					
8 dates Ⓓ 6.3.42 – 8.10.42					
*** 2.5.41 < 53,000	100	180	300	450	600

E–092   TYPE 5. [1943 – 1944]

CENTRAL BANK OF IRELAND – Emergency Tracer Overprint Code
Joseph Brennan, J. J. McElligott.
ETO CODES: black Ⓝ   red Ⓡ   brown Ⓜ

			€					
Print: ~ 1,500,000				**VG**	**Fine**	**VF**	**EF**	**UNC**
18 Dates.				30	130	250	400	600
6 dates Ⓝ3.2.43 – 1.7.43								
6 dates Ⓡ14.8.43 – 12.1.44								
6 dates Ⓜ16.2.44 – 14.7.44								
**** 1.7.43				100	200	400	500	700
** 12.1.44				30	130	300	400	600
092SC. 13.5.06 Ⓝ SPECIMEN							*750*	*1000*

E–093   TYPE 6. [1945 – 1951]

CENTRAL BANK OF IRELAND – ETO Code discontinued
Joseph Brennan, J. J. McElligott.

	€				
Print: ~ 8,000,000		**VG**	**Fine**	**VF**	**EF**	**UNC**
88 Dates. 17.1.45 – 24.4.51		20	40	70	100	170
***24.4.51						
Variations Non-sequential dating.						
093SC. 13.5.06 SPECIMEN						*560*

E–094   TYPE 7. [1952 – 1953]

CENTRAL BANK OF IRELAND – Serial numbers extended
Joseph Brennan, J. J. McElligott.

	€				
Print: ~ 4,000,000		**VG**	**Fine**	**VF**	**EF**	**UNC**
5 Dates. 6.8.52 – 24.3.53		-	-	40	70	120
***24.3.53		25	50	90	120	150

E–095   TYPE 8. [1954 – 1955]

CENTRAL BANK OF IRELAND – Signature variation
J. J. McElligott, O. J. Redmond. "Rúnaí na Roinne Airgeadais"

	€				
Print: ~ 5,000,000		**VG**	**Fine**	**VF**	**EF**	**UNC**
3 Dates. 3.5.54 – 24.10.55		-	-	40	90	150
***15. 9.55						
095SC. 13.5.06 SPECIMEN						*560*

E–096   TYPE 9. [1956 – 1960]
CENTRAL BANK OF IRELAND – Signature variation
J. J. McElligott, T. K. Whitaker.

		€			
Print: ~ 10,000,000		**VG**	**Fine**	**VF**	**EF**	**UNC**
5 Dates. 20.8.56 – 12.5.60		-	-	25	60	100
096SC. 13.5.06 SPECIMEN						*560*

E–097   TYPE 11. [1961 – 1968]
CENTRAL BANK OF IRELAND – Signature variation
"STERLING" promise dropped
M. Ó Muimhneacháin, T. K. Whitaker.

		€			
Print: ~ 37,400,000		**VG**	**Fine**	**VF**	**EF**	**UNC**
8 Dates. 15.8.61 – 12.8.68		-	-	20	40	100
Varieties: 12.6.68 Small date typeface.		-	-	20	40	100
+Variations: 15.8.61, 30.5.62, 20.6.63 **Mulberry.		-	35	60	180	200
097SC. 20.10.03 SPECIMEN						*560*
097SP1. 2.3.02 SPECIMEN						*260*
097SP2. various issued note dates SPECIMEN						*260*

E–098   TYPE 12. [1969 – 1970]
CENTRAL BANK OF IRELAND – Signature variation
T. K. Whitaker, C. H. Murray.

		€			
Print: 14,250,000		**VG**	**Fine**	**VF**	**EF**	**UNC**
2 Dates. 12.5.69 – 27.2.70		-	-	13	40	100
Varieties: 12.5.69 Small date typeface.						

E–099   TYPE 13 [1971 – 1975]
CENTRAL BANK OF IRELAND – Metallic security thread introduced
T. K. Whitaker, C. H. Murray.

		€			
Print: ~ 73,000,000		**VG**	**Fine**	**VF**	**EF**	**UNC**
6 Dates 18.1.71 – 5.9.75		-	-	10	30	70
2 Replacements. R		-	15	50	150	220
00K		-	-	30	80	180
Varieties: 26.5.74, 5.9.75 Sans-serif serial typeface.						
099SC. 2.5.05 SPECIMEN, dated 04.3.73						*560*

A full list of all observed replacement note dates along with known serial number brackets may be viewed on *http://www.irishpapermoney.com/replacements/star0.html*

Ten Pound Notes
1928 – 1976

**E–100   TYPE 1. [1928]
CURRENCY COMMISSION IRISH FREE STATE – Fractional prefix
Joseph Brennan, J. J. McElligott.

	Poor	VG	Fine	VF	EF	UNC
Print: ~ 450,000						€
1 Date. 10.9.28	100	500	1200	2000	3000	4000
100SC. 13.5.06 SPECIMEN						*1300*

**E–101   TYPE 2. [1932 – 1933]
CURRENCY COMMISSION IRISH FREE STATE – Linear prefix
Joseph Brennan, J. J. McElligott.

	VG	Fine	VF	EF	UNC
Print: ≤ 230,000					€
2 Dates. 6.7.32 – 16.1.33	100	150	500	1200	1500
***16.1.33					

E–102   TYPE 3. [1938 – 1940]
CURRENCY COMMISSION IRELAND
Joseph Brennan, J. J. McElligott. "Rúnaidhe na Roinne Airgeadais"

		VG	Fine	VF	EF	UNC
Print: ≥ 380,000						€
6 Dates. 27.10.38 – 2.7.40	1938	30	90	300	450	750
	1940	30	90	250	400	500

E–103   TYPE 4. [1941 – 1942]
CURRENCY COMMISSION IRELAND – Emergency Tracer Overprint Code
Joseph Brennan, J J McElligott.
ETO CODES: brown Ⓔ   grey-green Ⓕ

	VG	Fine	VF	EF	UNC
Print: ≥ 500,000					€
8 Dates.	50	100	380	550	850
4 dates Ⓔ 9.10.41 – 6.1.42					
4 dates Ⓕ 18.7.42 – 5.10.42					
**9.10.41	70	150	450	600	900
***6.1.42, 5.10.42	100	250	500	650	1000

E–104   **TYPE 5. [1943 – 1944]**
CENTRAL BANK OF IRELAND – Emergency Tracer Overprint Code
Joseph Brennan, J. J. McElligott.
ETO CODES: orange Ⓢ blue Ⓦ purple Ⓑ dark olive Ⓖ

		€	VG	Fine	VF	EF	UNC
Print: ~ 1,200,000			50	100	380	550	850
16 Dates.							
4 dates Ⓢ 2.3.43 – 8.6.43							
4 dates Ⓦ 23.9.43 – 28.12.43							
4 dates Ⓑ 3.2.44 – 16.5.44							
4 dates Ⓖ 9.9.44 – 11.12.44							
**8.6.43			70	150	450	600	900
***28.12.43, 16.5.44, 11.12.44			100	250	500	650	1000
104SC. 13.5.06 Ⓢ SPECIMEN							*1300*

E–105   **TYPE 6. [1945 – 1952]**
CENTRAL BANK OF IRELAND – ETO Code dropped
Joseph Brennan, J. J. McElligott.

		€	VG	Fine	VF	EF	UNC
Print: ~ 4,200,000							
48 Dates. 6.9.45 – 11.11.52	1945 – 1947		20	35	60	180	280
	1948 – 1952		18	25	50	120	220
**4.11.46, 11.11.52							
105SC. 13.5.06 SPECIMEN							*700*

E–106 TYPE 8. [1954 – 1955]

CENTRAL BANK OF IRELAND – Signature variation

J. J. McElligott, O. J. Redmond. "Rúnaí na Roinne Airgeadais"

Print: ≤ 940,000

	VG	Fine	€ VF	EF	UNC
11 Dates. 3.12.54 – 21.10.55	20	50	100	180	300
106SC. 13.5.06 SPECIMEN					*700*

E–107 TYPE 9. [1957 – 1960]

CENTRAL BANK OF IRELAND – Signature variation

J. J. McElligott, T. K. Whitaker.

Print: ~ 1,200,000

	VG	Fine	€ VF	EF	UNC
12 Dates. 7.1.57 – 14.1.60	-	20	40	70	150
***14.1.60	30	100			

E–108 TYPE 10. [1960]

CENTRAL BANK OF IRELAND – Serial numbers extended

J. J. McElligott, T. K. Whitaker.

Print: ~ 1,500,000

	VG	Fine	€ VF	EF	UNC
15 Dates. 9.2.60 – 6.12.60	-	20	40	70	150

E-109   TYPE 11. [1962 – 1968]

CENTRAL BANK OF IRELAND – Signature variation
                        "STERLING" promise dropped
M. Ó Muimhneacháin, T. K. Whitaker.

Print: ≥ 6,000,000	VG	Fine	€ VF	EF	UNC
9 Dates. 2.5.62 – 16.7.68	-	20	40	70	180
**5.2.64					
Varieties: 16.7.68 Small date typeface.					
Variations: 2.5.62, 17.5.62, 29.5.62 **Mulberry.	-	40	110	150	300
109SC. 2.3.02 SPECIMEN					*700*
109SP1. 2.3.02 SPECIMEN					*260*
109SP2. various issued note dates SPECIMEN					*260*

E-110   TYPE 12. [1969 – 1970]

CENTRAL BANK OF IRELAND – Signature variation
T. K. Whitaker, C, H. Murray.

Print: 3,500,000	VG	Fine	€ VF	EF	UNC
2 Dates. 5.5.69 – 9.3.70	-	-	40	70	180
Varieties: 5.5.69 Small date typeface.					

E-111   TYPE 13. [1971 – 1975]

CENTRAL BANK OF IRELAND – Metallic security thread introduced
T. K. Whitaker, C. H. Murray.

Print: ≥ 34,500,000	VG	Fine	€ VF	EF	UNC
5 Dates. 19.5.71 – 10.2.75	-	-	30	60	140
1 Replacement. 10.2.75 *T	-	-	50	150	250
Varieties: 26.9.74 Sans-serif serial typeface.					
111SC. 2.5.04 SPECIMEN, dated 04.3.73					*700*

E-112   TYPE 14. [1976]

CENTRAL BANK OF IRELAND – Signature variation
C. H. Murray, M. O Murchú.

Print: 10,000,000	VG	Fine	€ VF	EF	UNC
1 Date. 2.12.76	-	-	30	60	100
Replacement. *T	-	-	30	150	250

Illustrated, the only known example of an Irish Terminator 'one million note', with a hand-set seven digit 1000000 serial number.

Twenty Pound Notes
1928 – 1976

***E–113 TYPE 1. [1928]

CURRENCY COMMISSION IRISH FREE STATE – Fractional prefix
Joseph Brennan, J. J. McElligott.

Print: 47,000
1 Date.   10.9.28
113SC.   13.5.06   SPECIMEN

	Poor	VG	Fine	VF	EF	UNC
	200	1800	2400	3000	5000	–
						2000

€

E–114   TYPE 5. [1943 – 1944]
****

CENTRAL BANK OF IRELAND – Emergency Tracer Overprint Code – Linear prefix
Joseph Brennan, J. J. McElligott. "Rúnaidhe na Roinne Airgeadais"
ETO CODE: dark blue Ⓐ

Print: 33,000
11 dates Ⓐ 11.2.43 – 10.1.44
114SC.   13.5.06 Ⓐ SPECIMEN

	Poor	VG	Fine	VF	EF	UNC
	800	2300	3000	4200	–	–
						2000

€

E–115   TYPE 6. [1945 – 1952]

CENTRAL BANK OF IRELAND – ETO Code discontinued
Joseph Brennan, J. J. McElligott.

Print: ~ 580,000
70 Dates. 17.10.45 – 25.3.52

		Poor	VG	Fine	VF	EF	UNC
***1945 – 1946		70	100	300	600	850	1500
**1947 – 1948		50	90	150	500	750	1500
*1949		40	90	150	350	750	1500
1951 – 1952		40	80	100	300	650	1500
115SC. 13.5.06 SPECIMEN							*900*

E–116   TYPE 8. [1954 – 1955]

CENTRAL BANK OF IRELAND – Signature variation
J. J. McElligott, O. J. Redmond. "Rúnaí na Roinne Airgeadais"

Print: ~ 400,000
2 Dates. 27.4.54 – 2.9.55

	VG	Fine	VF	EF	UNC
	80	100	300	650	1500
116SC 13.5.06 SPECIMEN					*900*

E–117   TYPE 9. [1957]

CENTRAL BANK OF IRELAND – Signature variation
J. J. McElligott, T. K. Whitaker.

Print: ~ 200,000
1 Date. 23.10.57

	VG	Fine	VF	EF	UNC
	35	80	300	650	1500

E–118   TYPE 11. [1961 – 1965]

CENTRAL BANK OF IRELAND – Signature variation
                                    "STERLING" promise dropped
M. Ó Muimhneacháin, T. K. Whitaker.

Print: ≥ 1,150,000
4 Dates. 1.6.61 – 15.6.65

	VG	Fine	VF	EF	UNC
	-	60	120	250	500
118SC. 16.1.01 SPECIMEN					*900*
118SP1. 16.1.01 SPECIMEN					*700*
118SP2. various issued note dates SPECIMEN					*550*

E–119   TYPE 12. [1969 – 1975]

CENTRAL BANK OF IRELAND – Signature variation
T. K. Whitaker, C. H. Murray.

Print: ~ 3,400,000
6 Dates. 3.3.69 – 6.1.75   1970 – 1973

	VG	Fine	VF	EF	UNC
6 Dates. 3.3.69 – 6.1.75 1970 – 1973	-	40	90	150	300
Varieties: 3.3.69 Small date typeface. 1969	-	40	90	180	450
6.1.75 Sans-serif serial typeface. 1975	-	40	70	100	300
119SC1. 2.5.05 SPECIMEN, dated 04.3.73					*900*
119SC2. 3.3.69 SPECIMEN, dated 07.4.73					*900*

E–120   TYPE 14. [1976]

CENTRAL BANK OF IRELAND – Signature variation
C. H. Murray, M. O Murchú.

Print: ~ 5,400,000
1 Date. 24.3.76

	VG	Fine	VF	EF	UNC
1 Date. 24.3.76	-	40	70	100	300
Replacement. **V	50	150	300	500	1500
+Variations: Carmine blank.					

Fifty Pound Notes
1928 – 1977

E–121   **TYPE 1. [1928]**
****

CURRENCY COMMISSION IRISH FREE STATE – Fractional prefix
Joseph Brennan, J. J. McElligott.

		Poor	VG	Fine	VF	EF	UNC
Print: ~ 12,000						€	
1 Date.	10.9.28	400	3000	4000	6000	15000	18000
121SC.	13.5.06 SPECIMEN					*1800*	*2800*

E–122   **TYPE 6. [1943 – 1951]

CENTRAL BANK OF IRELAND – Linear prefix
Joseph Brennan, J. J. McElligott. "Rúnaidhe na Roinne Airgeadais"

		Poor	VG	Fine	VF	EF	UNC
Print: ~ 33,000						€	
33 Dates. 23.3.43 – 13.2.51	1946 – 1951	80	500	750	1200	1800	2500
	***1943	130	750	1000	1600	2200	3500
122SC.	13.5.06 SPECIMEN						*1000*

***E–123   **TYPE 8. [1954]**

CENTRAL BANK OF IRELAND – Signature variation
J. J. McElligott, O. J. Redmond. "Rúnaí na Roinne Airgeadais"

		Poor	VG	Fine	VF	EF	UNC
Print: ~ 10,000						€	
2 Dates.	22.4.54 – 4.5.54	80	600	800	1500	2000	2800
123SC.	13.5.06 SPECIMEN						*1000*

SPECIMEN banknotes are known for most Types of Legal Tender Notes. There are two varieties, Specimens of the Issuing Authority identified in this book by SC suffixed to the catalogue number, and De La Rue Printer's Specimens identified by SP suffix.

**E–124 TYPE 9. [1957 – 1960]

CENTRAL BANK OF IRELAND – Signature variation
J. J. McElligott, T. K. Whitaker.

Print: ~ 20,000

	VG	Fine	VF	EF	UNC
2 Dates. 4.10.57 – 16.5.60	400	600	1300	1600	2500

E–125 TYPE 11. [1962 – 1968]

CENTRAL BANK OF IRELAND – Signature variation
"STERLING" promise dropped
M. Ó Muimhneacháin, T. K. Whitaker.

Print: ~ 47,000

		VG	Fine	VF	EF	UNC
4 Dates. 1.2.62 – 6.9.68	1962 – 1963	130	300	450	600	1100
** 11.7.66	1966	130	300	500	650	1200
Variations: 1.2.62 **Mulberry.		130	300	550	800	1300
Varieties: 6.9.68 Small date typeface.	1968	130	300	350	450	1000
125SC. 2.3.02 SPECIMEN						*1000*
125SP. various issued note dates SPECIMEN						*700*

E–126 TYPE 12. [1970 – 1975]

CENTRAL BANK OF IRELAND – Signature variation
T. K. Whitaker, C. H. Murray.

Print: ~ 100,000

		VG	Fine	VF	EF	UNC
5 Dates. 4.11.70 – 16.4.75	1970 – 1971	130	250	350	450	1000
	1972 – 1975	130	250	300	400	700
+Varieties: 16.4.75 Sans-serif serial typeface.						
126SC1. 2.5.05 SPECIMEN, dated 03.3.73						*1000*
126SC2. 00.1.00 SPECIMEN, sans-serif						*1000*

E–127 TYPE 14. [1977]

CENTRAL BANK OF IRELAND – Signature variation.
C H Murray, M O Murchú.

Print: ~ 1,000,000

	VG	Fine	VF	EF	UNC
1 Date. 4.4.77	130	250	300	400	800

NOTE: The illustrated £50 note, 20.2.73 03Y 023000 is the last Legal Tender £50 note to be printed by De La Rue. All subsequent notes were printed in Sandyford by The Central Bank of Ireland.

One Hundred Pound Notes
1928 – 1977

E–128   TYPE 1. [1928]
****

CURRENCY COMMISSION IRISH FREE STATE – Fractional prefix
Joseph Brennan, J. J. McElligott.

Print: ≤ 4,000
   1 Date. 10.9.28
   128CS. **13.5.06** SPECIMEN.

	Poor	VG	Fine	VF	EF	UNC
	400	3000	4000	6000	15000	18000
					1250	1800

***E–129   Type 2. [1937]

CURRENCY COMMISSION IRISH FREE STATE – Linear prefix
Joseph Brennan, J. J. McElligott.

Print: 6,300
   4 Dates. 9.12.37 – 20.12.37
   **** 20.12.37

	P	VG	Fine	VF	EF	UNC
	200	1300	1800	3000	6000	8000

E–130 TYPE 6. [1943 – 1949]
CENTRAL BANK OF IRELAND
Joseph Brennan, J. J. McElligott. "Rúnaidhe na Roinne Airgeadais" €

		P	VG	Fine	VF	EF	UNC
Print: ~ 23,000							
24 Dates. 3.2.43 – 3.9.49	1946 - 1949	–	260	600	1000	1600	2200
	**1943	160	350	1000	1300	2200	3500
130SC. 13.5.06 SPECIMEN							*1000*

E–131 TYPE 8. [1954]
CENTRAL BANK OF IRELAND – Signature variation
J. J. McElligott, O. J. Redmond. "Rúnaí na Roinne Airgeadais" €

	VG	Fine	VF	EF	UNC
Print: ≥ 11,000					
2 Dates. 21.4.54 – 1.5.54	200	500	1000	1600	2000
131SC. 13.5.06 SPECIMEN					*1000*

E–132 Type 9. [1959]
CENTRAL BANK OF IRELAND – Signature variation
J. J. McElligott, T. K. Whitaker. €

	VG	Fine	VF	EF	UNC
Print: ≥ 13,000					
2 Dates. 14.10.59 – 11.11.59	200	500	850	1400	2000

E–133 Type 11. [1963 – 1968]
CENTRAL BANK OF IRELAND – Signature variation
                              "STERLING" promise dropped.
M. Ó Muimhneacháin, T. K. Whitaker. €

	VG	Fine	VF	EF	UNC
Print: > 40,000					
5 Dates. 16.1.63 – 9.9.68	190	300	450	1000	1200
Varieties: 9.9.68 Small date typeface.					
Variations: 16.1.63, 21.11.63 **Mulberry.	230	400	600	1200	1400
133SC. 2.3.02 SPECIMEN					*1000*
133SP. various issued note dates SPECIMEN					*700*

E–134 Type 12. [1970 – 1973]
CENTRAL BANK OF IRELAND – Signature variation
T. K. Whitaker, C. H. Murray. €

		VG	Fine	VF	EF	UNC
Print: ~ 200,000						
4 Dates. 26.10.70 – 10.4.75	1970	190	300	450	900	1000
	1972 – 1973	190	300	400	550	900
	1975	190	300	400	550	900
+Varieties: 10.4.75 Sans-serif serial typeface.						
134SC1. 26.10.70 SPECIMEN						*1000*
134SC2. 2.5.05 SPECIMEN, dated 04.3.73						*1000*

E–135 TYPE 14. [1977]
CENTRAL BANK OF IRELAND – Signature variation
C. H. Murray, M. O Murchú. €

	VG	Fine	VF	EF	UNC
Print: ~ 500,000 (300,000 were probably not issued)					
1 Date. 4.4.77	190	300	400	550	900

A Series Banknotes
Year Chart

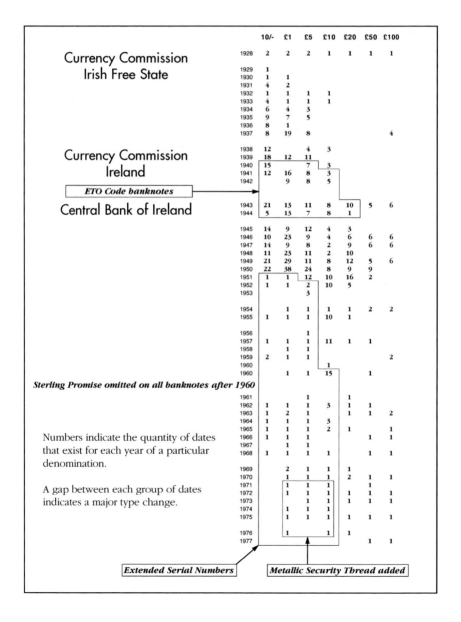

Issuer / Notes	Year	10/-	£1	£5	£10	£20	£50	£100
Currency Commission Irish Free State	1928	2	2	2	1	1	1	1
	1929	1						
	1930	1	1					
	1931	4	2					
	1932	1	1	1	1			
	1933	4	1	1	1			
	1934	6	4	3				
	1935	9	7	5				
	1936	8	1					
	1937	8	19	8				4
Currency Commission Ireland	1938	12		4	3			
	1939	18	12	11				
	1940	15		7	3			
	1941	12	16	8	3			
	1942		9	8	5			
ETO Code banknotes →								
Central Bank of Ireland	1943	21	13	11	8	10	5	6
	1944	5	13	7	8	1		
	1945	14	9	12	4	3		
	1946	10	23	9	4	6	6	6
	1947	14	9	8	2	9	6	6
	1948	11	23	11	2	10		
	1949	21	29	11	8	12	5	6
	1950	22	38	24	8	9	9	
	1951	1	1	12	10	16	2	
	1952	1	1	2	10	5		
	1953			3				
	1954		1	1	1	1	2	2
	1955	1	1	1	10	1		
	1956			1				
	1957	1	1	1	11	1	1	
	1958		1	1				
	1959	2	1	1				2
	1960				1			
	1960		1	1	15		1	
	1961			1		1		
	1962	1	1	1	3	1	1	
	1963	1	2	1		1	1	2
	1964	1	1	1	3			
	1965	1	1	1	2	1		1
	1966	1	1	1			1	1
	1967		1	1				
	1968	1	1	1	1		1	1
	1969		2	1	1	1		
	1970		1	1	1	2	1	1
	1971		1	1	1		1	
	1972		1	1	1	1	1	1
	1973			1	1	1	1	1
	1974		1	1	1			
	1975		1	1	1	1	1	1
	1976		1		1	1		
	1977			1		1	1	1

Sterling Promise omitted on all banknotes after 1960

Numbers indicate the quantity of dates that exist for each year of a particular denomination.

A gap between each group of dates indicates a major type change.

Extended Serial Numbers

Metallic Security Thread added

Section 3

Irish Government Banknotes

Central Bank of Ireland
Legal Tender B Series Banknotes
1976 – 1993

One Pound Notes
1977 – 1989

E–136   **TYPE 16. [1977]**
CENTRAL BANK OF IRELAND
C. H. Murray, M. O Murchú.

			€		
Print: 64,000,000	VG	Fine	VF	EF	UNC
6 Dates. 10.06.77 – 29.11.77	-	-	-	5	15
4 Replacements. BBB	-	-	8	30	80

E–137   **TYPE 17. [1978 – 1981]**
CENTRAL BANK OF IRELAND – Signature variation
C. H. Murray, Tomás F. Ó Cofaigh.

			€		
Print: 272,000,000	VG	Fine	VF	EF	UNC
23 Dates. 30.08.78 – 30.10.81	-	-	-	5	15
+12 Replacements. BBB, DDD, GGG	-	-	8	30	80

E–138   **TYPE 18. [1982 – 1987]**
CENTRAL BANK OF IRELAND – Signature variation
Tomás F. Ó Cofaigh, Maurice F. Doyle.

			€		
Print: 353,000,000	VG	Fine	VF	EF	UNC
30 Dates. 30.06.82 – 24.04.87	-	-	-	5	10
+12 Replacements. GGG, BBB	-	-	8	30	80
138S. 00.00.00 SPECIMEN					

E–139   **TYPE 19. [1988 – 1989]**
CENTRAL BANK OF IRELAND – Signature variation
Maurice F. Doyle, S. P. Cromien.

			€		
Print: 120,000,000	VG	Fine	VF	EF	UNC
9 Dates. 23.03.88 – 17.07.89	-	-	-	5	10
4 Replacements. BBB	-	-	8	20	70

SPECIMEN banknotes were produced for each change of signature with varying prefixes of three letters the same, not necessarily being those employed on replacements of the same denomination. Those that have been observed to date are listed.

A full list of all observed replacement note dates along with known serial number brackets may be viewed on *http://www.irishpapermoney.com/replacements/star0.html*

Five Pound Notes
1976 – 1993

E–140   **Type 15. [1976]**
CENTRAL BANK OF IRELAND
T. K. Whitaker, C. H. Murray.

				€		
Print: 8,000,000		VG	Fine	VF	EF	UNC
1 Date. 26.02.76		-	-	10	20	70
Replacement. AAA		-	-	30	100	180

E–141   **Type 16. [1976 – 1977]**
CENTRAL BANK OF IRELAND – Signature variation
C. H. Murray, M. O Murchú.

				€		
Print: ~ 54,500,000		VG	Fine	VF	EF	UNC
5 Dates. 18.05.76 – 17.10.77		-	-	-	15	40
2 Replacements. AAA		-	-	13	50	130

E–142   **Type 17. [1979 – 1981]**
CENTRAL BANK OF IRELAND – Signature variation
C. H. Murray, Tomás F. Ó Cofaigh.

				€		
Print: ~ 99,500,000		VG	Fine	VF	EF	UNC
9 Dates. 25.04.79 – 29.10.81		-	-	-	15	40
4 Replacements. AAA		-	-	13	50	130

E–143   **Type 18. [1983 – 1987]**
CENTRAL BANK OF IRELAND – Signature variation
Tomás F. Ó Cofaigh, Maurice F. Doyle.

				€		
Print: ~ 109,500,000		VG	Fine	VF	EF	UNC
7 Dates. 17.10.83 – 22.04.87		-	-	-	15	30
5 Replacements. AAA		-	-	13	50	130
143S. 00.00.00 SPECIMEN						600

E–144   **Type 19. [1988 – 1993]**
CENTRAL BANK OF IRELAND – Signature variation
Maurice F. Doyle, S. P. Cromien.

				€		
Print: 153,000,000		VG	Fine	VF	EF	UNC
14 Dates. 12.08.88 – 07.05.93		-	-	-	10	30
3 Replacements. AAA		-	-	13	50	130
FFF		-	-	13	30	100

59

Ten Pound Notes
1978 – 1992

E–1 45   **Type 17. [1978 – 1981]**
CENTRAL BANK OF IRELAND
C. H. Murray, Tomás F. Ó Cofaigh.

	VG	Fine	€ VF	EF	UNC
Print: ~ 132,000,000	-	-	20	35	90
13 Dates. 01.06.78 – 28.10.81					
7 Replacements. CCC	-	30	70	150	300

E–146   **Type 18. [1983 – 1987]**
CENTRAL BANK OF IRELAND – Signature variation
Tomás F. Ó Cofaigh, Maurice F. Doyle.

	VG	Fine	€ VF	EF	UNC
Print: ~ 94,000,000	-	-	-	30	70
9 Dates. 25.02.83 – 09.02.87					
4 Replacements. HHH	-	30	70	150	300
146S. 00.00.00 SPECIMEN					

E–147   **Type 19. [1987 – 1992]**
CENTRAL BANK OF IRELAND – Signature variation
Maurice F. Doyle, S. P. Cromien.

	VG	Fine	€ VF	EF	UNC
Print: ~ 127,000,000	-	-	-	30	70
13 Dates. 22.12.87 – 15.04.92					
4 Replacements. HHH	-	30	70	150	300

Twenty Pound Notes
1980 – 1992

E–148   **Type 17. [1980 – 1981]**
CENTRAL BANK OF IRELAND – Signature variation
C. H. Murray, Tomás F. Ó Cofaigh.

	VG	Fine	€ VF	EF	UNC
Issue: ~ 36,800,000	-	-	40	80	120
4 Dates. 07.01.80 – 28.10.81	-	50	200	300	500
3 Replacements. EEE					

E–149   **Type 18. [1983 – 1986]**
CENTRAL BANK OF IRELAND – Signature variation
Tomás F. Ó Cofaigh, Maurice F. Doyle.

	VG	Fine	€ VF	EF	UNC
Print: 66,200,000	-	-	40	80	120
6 Dates. 11.07.83 – 28.08.86	-	50	250	300	500
4 Replacements. EEE					
149S. 00.00.00 SPECIMEN					600

E–150   **Type 19. [1987 – 1992]**
CENTRAL BANK OF IRELAND – Signature variation
Maurice F. Doyle, S. P. Cromien.

	VG	Fine	€ VF	EF	UNC
Print: 171,000,000		-	35	50	100
15 Dates. 12.08.87 – 14.02.92		50	250	300	500
5 Replacements. EEE, LLL		50	300	400	500
** LLL 06.02.89					

A full list of all observed replacement note dates along with known serial number brackets may be viewed on *http://www.irishpapermoney.com/replacements/star0.html*

Fifty Pound Notes
1982 – 1991

E–151 **TYPE 18. [1982]**
CENTRAL BANK OF IRELAND.
Tomás F. Ó Cofaigh, Maurice F. Doyle.

	VG	Fine	€ VF	EF	UNC
Print: 8,000,000					
1 Date. 01.11.82	-	75	85	100	250
*** Replacement. KKK	-	100	350	700	1800
151S. 00.00.00 SPECIMEN					600

E–152 **TYPE 19. [1991]**
CENTRAL BANK OF IRELAND – Signature variation
Maurice F. Doyle, S. P. Cromien.

	VG	Fine	€ VF	EF	UNC
Print: 5,000,000					
1 Date. 05.11.91	-	75	85	100	250
** Replacement. KKK	-	70	250	500	1000

Section 4

Irish Government Banknotes

Central Bank of Ireland
Legal Tender C Series Banknotes
1992 – 2001

Five Pound Notes
1994 – 1999

E–153   TYPE 20. [1994]
CENTRAL BANK OF IRELAND
Maurice F. Doyle, S. P. Cromien.

				€		
Print: 39,000,000		VG	Fine	VF	EF	UNC
4 Dates. 15.03.94 – 28.08.94		-	-	-	-	30
2 Replacements. HHH		-	-	-	25	70
153S. 00.00.00 HHH 000000 SPECIMEN						

E–154   TYPE 21. [1994 – 1997]
CENTRAL BANK OF IRELAND – Signature variation
Position of tactile mark slightly modified
Muiris S. Ó Conaill, P. Mullarkey.

				€		
Print: 102,000,000.		VG	Fine	VF	EF	UNC
7 Dates. 21.12.94 – 14.02.97		-	-	-	-	30
2 Replacements. HHH		-	-	-	25	70

E–155   TYPE 22. [1998 – 1999]
CENTRAL BANK OF IRELAND – Alteration of Serial Prefixing Letters to M to Z
Letters O and Q are not used
Muiris S. Ó Conaill, P. Mullarkey.

				€		
Print: 105,000,000		VG	Fine	VF	EF	UNC
3 Dates. 19.08.98 – 15.10.99		-	-	-	-	20
2 Replacements. MMM		-	-	15	30	70

A full list of all observed replacement note dates along with known serial number brackets may be viewed on *http://www.irishpapermoney.com/replacements/star0.html*

Ten Pound Notes
1993 – 1999

E–156   TYPE 20. [1993 – 1994]
CENTRAL BANK OF IRELAND
S. P. Cromien, Maurice Doyle.

	VG	Fine	VF	EF	UNC
Print: 59,000,000					
5 Dates. 14.07.93 – 27.07.94	-	-	-	-	45
3 Replacements. J J J	-	-	-	30	100
**5Z2 J J J 687051 – J J J 786630	-	30	60	80	100
156S. 00.00.00 J J J 000000 SPECIMEN	-	-	-	-	*300*

E–157   TYPE 21. [1995 – 1997]
CENTRAL BANK OF IRELAND – Signature variation
Muiris S. Ó Conaill, P. Mullarkey.

	VG	Fine	VF	EF	UNC
Print: 99,000,000					
8 Dates. 13.03.95 – 06.05.97	-	-	-	-	45
4 Replacements. J J J	-	-	-	30	100

E–158   TYPE 22. [1997 – 1999]
CENTRAL BANK OF IRELAND – Alteration of Serial Prefixing Letters to M to Z
Letters O and Q are not used

Muiris S. Ó Conaill, P. Mullarkey.

	VG	Fine	VF	EF	UNC
Print: ~152,000,000					
7 Dates. 04.12.97 – 02.07.99	-	-	-	-	35
2 Replacements. NNN	-	-	-	25	70
Varieties: • Commencing from 02.02.98 Design B reverse.					

E-156 Type 20 replacement notes dated 27.07.94 occur in two distinct blocks as
follows: 5Z1.   J J J 240604 – J J J 293830
                 5Z2.   J J J 687051 – J J J 786630
Replacement notes in the gap between 5Z1 and 5Z2 occur with later dates on Type 21
notes. A likely explanation of this numbering pattern of replacements would be that a
small stock of Type 20 blank unnumbered notes were used up during the printage of
Type 21 notes. The only available prefix for these notes would have been the JJJ
replacement prefix. 5Z2 notes appeared in circulation during 1998.

+   Type 22 standard issue £10 notes dated 13.01.98 and replacement notes dated 24.03.98
appear with both design A and design B reverse.

Twenty Pound Notes
1992 – 1999

E–159 **TYPE 20. [1992 – 1994]**
CENTRAL BANK OF IRELAND
S. P. Cromien, Maurice F. Doyle.

	VG	Fine	VF	EF	UNC
Print: 141,000,000					
12 Dates². 10.09.92, 21.09.92 – 29.04.94	-	-	-	-	80
7 Replacements. BBB	-	-	30	60	250
**1Z. BBB Trial dated 10.9.92	30	40	70	300	500
**14.01.94 BBB	-	-	50	120	300
159S. 00.00.00 BBB 000000 SPECIMEN	-	-	-	-	*300*

E–160 **TYPE 21. [1995 – 1997]**
CENTRAL BANK OF IRELAND – Signature variation
Muiris S. Ó Conaill, P. Mullarkey.

	VG	Fine	VF	EF	UNC
Print: 164,000,000					
13 Dates. 14.06.95 – 02.09.97	-	-	-	-	50
6 Replacements. BBB, FFF, CCC	-	-	35	70	200

E–161 **TYPE 22. [1997 – 1999]**
CENTRAL BANK OF IRELAND – Alteration of Serial Prefixing Letters to M to Z
Letters O and Q are not used
Muiris S. Ó Conaill, P. Mullarkey.

	VG	Fine	VF	EF	UNC
Print: 238,000,000					
11 Dates. 23.09.97 – 09.12.99	-	-	-	-	55
4 Replacements³. P P P	-	-	50	80	200
Varieties: • Commencing from 29.10.97 Design B reverse.					

---

1. 1Z. 10.09.92. Probable trial of new note printing. Date printed only as a BBB replacement note, with a likely printage of 60,000 notes for the date in total.
2. E–159.11, 28.04.94. Prefixes BAI, CAI, EAI, FAI, HAI are shared with the date of issue following it, E–159.12, 29.04.94.
3. Contrary to what has been stated as fact elsewhere (*"Paper Money of Ireland"*, by Blake & Calloway, 2009, page 454.) VVV prefix was almost certainly not used as a Replacement prefix in Type 22 £20 notes.

Fifty Pound Notes
1995 – 2001

E–162   **TYPE 21. [1995 – 1996]**
CENTRAL BANK OF IRELAND
Muiris S. Ó Conaill, P. Mullarkey.

	VG	Fine	VF	EF	UNC
Print: 12,000,000	-	-	-	-	200
2 Dates. 06.10.95 – 14.02.96					
2 Replacements. EEE	-	-	130	250	450
Variations: 1A. Low Tactile mark on earlier notes.					

€

E–164   **TYPE 22. [1999]**
CENTRAL BANK OF IRELAND – **Alteration of Serial Prefixing Letters to M to Z**
Letters O and Q are not used
New design security thread introduced.
Muiris S. Ó Conaill, P. Mullarkey.

€

	VG	Fine	VF	EF	UNC
Print: 28,000,000	-	-	-	-	180
1 Date. 19.03.99					
1 Replacement. RRR	-	-	-	130	280

E–165   **TYPE 23. [2001]**
CENTRAL BANK OF IRELAND – **"Ard-Rúnaí na Roinne Airgeadais"**
Muiris S. Ó Conaill, John A. Hurley.

€

	VG	Fine	VF	EF	UNC
Print: ~23,000,000 (ZRR not seen)	-	-	-	-	200
1 Date. 08.03.01					

+   E-165. Irish language title of Secretary of the Department of Finance changes to
"Ard-Rúnaí na Roinne Airgeadais" from "Rúnaí na Roinne Airgeadais" on earlier notes.
1.   Contrary to what has been stated as fact elsewhere (*"Paper Money of Ireland"*, by Blake &
Calloway, 2009, page 454.) EEE is highly unlikely to have been used as a replacement prefix for
Type 22 £50 notes, considering that Type 22 £50 notes use _ _ R as a series base letter and are
printed under the M to Z prefixing group. Both of these facts, especially the latter, absolutely
preclude the use of EEE as a replacement identifier for £50 notes dated 19.03.99.

One Hundred Pound Notes

1996

E–163 **TYPE 21. [1996]**

CENTRAL BANK OF IRELAND

Muiris S Ó Conaill, P Mullarkey.

	VG	Fine	€ VF	EF	UNC
Print: ~ 5,000,000 (1,000,000 or more not issued)					
1 Date. 22.08.96	-	-	-	160	450
Replacement. KKK	-	170	200	250	700

The numbering system established in *"Irish Banknotes – Irish Government Paper Money from 1928"*, published in 1999 has been retained without any changes in order to prevent possible confusion between that book and this one.

Visit
www.irishpapermoney.com
for an on-line museum of Irish banknotes
from ca. 1800 – 2001

Section 5

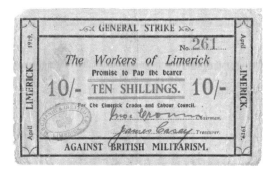

ANCILLARY
BANKNOTE ISSUES

BANKNOTES OF THE LIMERICK SOVIET
April, 1919

Background to the Limerick Soviet Banknote Issues

1919

Industrial Unrest

The aftermath of the 1916 Rising had removed most of the militant Nationalist leaders from circulation. This allowed the rise of the militant labour movement, sometimes in an unsure alliance with the new Sinn Féin movement.

With a shortage of troops for the war in Europe, the British Government decided to extend conscription to Ireland in April, 1918. Politicians, the Church and the labour movement, in the form of the ITGWU, all came together in their opposition to conscription. This resulted in a general strike in protest on 23 April 1918 which lead to the idea of conscription in Ireland being abandoned, a significant victory over the British Government.

At the end of World War 1 Europe was in turmoil. Germany and the Austro-Hungarian Empire had collapsed, taking the old order with them, against the background of the rise of Bolshevism. There was widespread social and economic revolution throughout the continent. In the United Kingdom of Great Britain and Ireland there was similar unrest with regular strikes in major industrial cities in Britain. August 1918 to April 1919 saw general strikes in several locations in Ireland in a peaceful effort to win a better deal for workers. This was against a general background of insurrection in Ireland as the War of Independence commenced.

The lead up to the strike

It was against this background that an incident occurred on 6 April 1919 in which Robert Byrne, a trade unionist and IRA man, court martialed and jailed in February on a gun possession charge, was rescued by the IRA from a prison hospital. It was a botched operation, during which a police constable, Martin O'Brien, was killed. Byrne also died later from his wounds. He had been a leader of the struggle for political status for IRA prisoners whilst in prison. Thousands of marchers attended his funeral on April 10.

Martial Law

On April 9, citing the death of the police constable as a reason, much of Limerick city and county was declared a Special Military Area under the provisions of the Defence of the Realm Act. These provisions were intended to flush out IRA men concealed in the midst of local populations. It enabled the military to issue exit and entry permits for the area and made the population subject to police inspections at any time. Tanks were used to secure the streets at entry points to the SMA. The restrictions were quite repressive and were resented by the population at large.

The Strike

The Limerick Trades and Labour Council was an umbrella organisation of 35 trade unions. It's president was John Cronin of the Amalgamated Society of Carpenters. At a meeting on Sunday April 13 1919, the LTLC called a general strike in Limerick, to protest at martial law and the fact that many workers had to have permits and pass through the military check points in order to go to and from work each day. The strike started on Monday 14 April 1919. 14,000 workers had joined the strike by that Monday evening.

The strike committee took over the administration of Limerick, a city of 38,000. The distribution of food throughout the city was regulated and prices were strictly controlled to avoid shortages or profiteering. Certain shops were instructed to be open between 2 and 5 pm each day to supply foodstuffs to the population. The LTLC also published its own newspaper and issued its own currency. It quickly became known as the Limerick Soviet, although the situation bore little in common with happenings in Russia.

The resolution of the strike

Negotiations progressed throughout the duration of the strike. The British Army softened the regulations governing the issue of permits, by suggesting that employers be allowed to issue them, a move rejected in the first instance by the Soviet's leaders. In the end, the strike was not supported by other unions outside of the Limerick area, most notably the big unions based in Britain. The hope of its organisers that it might become a country-wide general strike, or that Limerick cuated, were not realised, leaving the strikers few options but to accept a settlement. The LTLC decided to end the strike and on Friday 25 April most strikers resumed work, only those subject to permit inspections remaining out. The strike ended on Monday 28 April with all the strikers returning to work.

In the event, any IRA men who were within the SMA kept a low profile throughout the proceedings and it proved ineffective in its efforts to flush them out. On 5 May Military restrictions were officially ended.

The British Army commander in charge of the military area was a General Griffin, who handled the

70

whole affair with cautious but firm diplomacy and sought to avoid any nasty incidents. On the whole, the affair was a generally peaceful one. The only significant confrontation was the eventual successful breach of the area by several hundred people on Easter Monday, 21 April 1919, following a protest the day before.

Although an open challenge to the British Government, the strike was not intended to be political, but was about the rights of workers to come and go to their place of work without repression.

The banknote issue

Some unions, most notably the National Union of Railwaymen, decided not to issue strike pay to their striking members inside the Soviet. Although food was sent in sizable quantities from the outside, little money was forthcoming. The resulting shortage of money in circulation lead the Soviet to take the decision to issue its own currency in the form of banknotes.

Security for the note issue was in the first instance to be the food stocks sent free from outside and the financial support of the workers of Limerick. Later, the notes were backed by the trades council and the Trade Union Congress, and by the approved shops which agreed to accept them. The banknote issue proved to be a stable one.

A sub-committee of the LTLC propaganda committee was in charge of printing and issuing the currency. The size of the population would suggest the need for a substantial banknote issue. Available data suggests that the entire issue was redeemed by the LTLC. A small surplus of unredeemed banknotes remained in a fund that had been subscribed to by sympathisers throughout Ireland. Some of these notes were probably kept as souvenirs.

Signature varieties

There are two suggestions as to why more than one signature variety exists. The first suggestion is that a proxy signature system was in use during the issue period of the notes whereby, others signed the notes in the name of the signatories with their agreement. The second suggestion is that unissued notes were signed after the end of the strike, by persons other than the signatories, for souvenir hunters. If the latter is the case, then the notes with the non-standard signatures may be regarded as at best an extraordinary issue, or at worst being non-valid due to a lack of an authorised signature.

Currently there are three versions of the signature pair known. Two examples of one of the versions, B2, have been observed on un-numbered notes, which might suggest a post-strike souvenir notes. Version B1 has been observed on numbered notes, suggesting an official proxy signature during the strike. Version A is in the hand of the signatories themselves and therefore definitely the official issue.

> ### Further Reading
>
> A comprehensive book on the Limerick Soviet was written by Liam Cahill in 1990:
> "Forgotten Revolution – Limerick Soviet 1919" ISBN 0-86278-194-9. For those interested in the full story this book is highly recommended.
> Also, visit *www.limericksoviet.com* for more information.

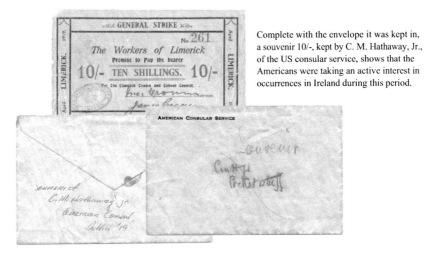

Complete with the envelope it was kept in, a souvenir 10/-, kept by C. M. Hathaway, Jr., of the US consular service, shows that the Americans were taking an active interest in occurrences in Ireland during this period.

One Series. [1919] The Limerick Trades and Labour Council

The Workers of Limerick General Strike against British Militarism.
Purple Mechanics Institute of Limerick oval shamrock stamp on lower left of each note.

Four Types:
    A1. Signatures **John Cronin** *Chairman,* **James Casey** *Treasurer.*
    A2. Signatures as above, but banknote not stamped. 10/- No. 311
    B. Signed as the signatories but by persons other than the signatories.
    B1. Signatures **John Cronin** *Chairman,* **J. M.Casey** *Treasurer.*
        But authored by someone other than the signatories – numbered.
    B2. Signatures **John Cronin** *Chairman,* **James. M.Casey** *Treasurer.*
        A different proxy author – un-numbered. This may be an example of an unissued note
        signed after the conclusion of the strike and kept as a souvenir.
    C. Signed backwards by a single person as
        James Casey *Chairman,* **John Cronin** *Treasurer.*
    D. Unsigned but numbered and stamped. Possibly unissued notes awaiting signatures.

LK–1   1 Shilling notes [1919]

ONE SHILLING in grey in the centre of the note

		€				
		VG	**Fine**	**VF**	**EF**	**UNC**
A.	Genuine Signatures. Numbers traced: 1 – 362	900	1200	1400	1600	1800
B1.	Proxy Signatures. Numbers traced: 307	900	1200	1400	1600	1800
D.	Unsigned, numbered. Numbers traced: 185, 341	900	1200	1400	1600	1800

LK–2   5 Shilling notes [1919]

FIVE SHILLINGS in green in the centre of the note

		€				
		VG	**Fine**	**VF**	**EF**	**UNC**
A.	Genuine Signatures. Numbers traced: 1 – 123	900	1200	1400	1600	1800
B1.	Proxy Signatures. Numbers traced: 167	900	1200	1400	1600	1800
C.	Signed Backwards. Numbers traced: 195	900	1200	1400	1600	1800

LK–3   10 Shilling notes [1919]

TEN SHILLINGS in red in the centre of the note

		€				
		VG	**Fine**	**VF**	**EF**	**UNC**
A.	Genuine Signatures. Numbers traced: 1 – 311	900	1200	1400	1600	1800
B2.	Proxy Signatures. Un-numbered: 5 notes	900	1200	1400	1600	1800

Type B1 note.

Type B2 note.

Type C note.

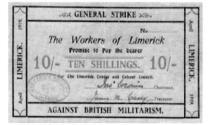

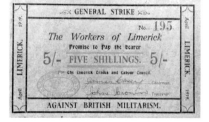

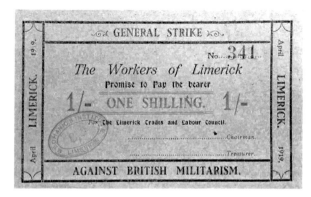

An example of a Type D 1/- note.

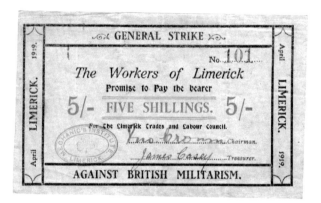

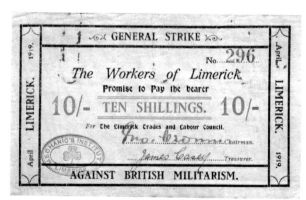

Examples of a Type A 5/- and 10/- notes.

Grading Banknotes

The "Fine" system of grading is that which is most widely in use currently. It is used in this book. There follows a brief description of each major grading term in the Fine system. This is intended as a guide, to assist a collector in learning to recognise the condition of a note. In addition to this, are some pointers on what to look out for when deciding the grade of a note, and how to spot attempted cleaning. The descriptions below are based on the IBNS standard grading definitions.

UNC (Uncirculated)
A perfectly preserved note, never mishandled by the Issuing Authority, a bank teller, the public or a collector. Paper is clean and firm, without discolouration. Corners are sharp and square, without any evidence of rounding. (Rounded corners are often a tell-tale sign of a cleaned or "doctored" note.) An uncirculated note will have its original natural sheen.

AU (About Uncirculated)
A virtually perfect note, with some minor handling. May show evidence of bank counting folds at a corner or one light fold through the centre, but not both. An AU note cannot be creased, a crease being a hard fold which has usually "broken" the surface of a note. Paper is clean and bright with original sheen. Corners are not rounded.

EF (Extremely Fine)
A very attractive note, with light handling. May have a maximum of three light folds or one strong crease. Paper is clean and bright with original sheen. Corners may show only the slightest evidence of rounding. There may also be the slightest sign of wear where a fold meets the edge.

VF (Very Fine)
Substantial signs of wear will be evident. The paper should however be crisp and firm, and there should be no surface damage. Multiple folds and creases, with wear on the corners. Slight surface dirt may also be present.

F (Fine)
The body of the banknote is relatively limp. The note is well circulated. Many folds, more than can be counted. The surface of the paper may be damaged due to wear along the heaviest fold. The corners may be rounded and damaged.

VG (Very Good)
Heavily worn and quite limp, small pieces may be missing from the margins of the note. Some of the creases will be worn heavily into the paper, causing surface damage. Parts of the fine print of texts may be indistinct. Tiny edge tears are inevitable and there may be a hole worn in the body of the note by folds meeting in the centre.

G (Good)
Good actually means the opposite! A damaged note with many tears, some into the design can be expected. Pieces may be missing, but no part of the printed design should be torn away.

Poor (P)
Only a rare note is collectable in this condition. With very bad damage, parts of the note which include the printed design may be missing. The note might also be torn into two parts and taped.

The raised intaglio printing of the title of the Issuing Authority and of the Signatures should always be detectable to the touch on an Irish banknote of grade VF or better.

Additions to grading terms
A system of plus and minus, or terms like "good", "almost", "choice" etc is used in combination with the descriptive terms to describe banknotes which fall in between these main terms. Dealers should always explain the terms they use. Any damage to a note, tears, washing, etc should be mentioned in addition to its grade.

Against Cleaning and Washing
A banknote which has been washed and or ironed (frequently referred to as having been "pressed") will appear with a dull, sometimes bright mat finish to its surface, which may also be abraded. If it has not been rinsed properly, then it could still reek of whatever detergent it was washed with. Ripples may be pressed into the paper where it has been dried unevenly. Do not however confuse the plastic smell of a polythene pocket (often used to store notes) with that of a detergent. Incidentally, polythene pockets are not recommended for note storage.

Being washed and or ironed is probably the worst of all the damages that a banknote can suffer. Washing a note irrevocably damages the structure of the paper and removes the sizing, a glossy protective coating on the surface. Cleaning can adversely affect the stability of the ink. It is akin to polishing a set of proof coins. The mood of the hobby is very much against this type of mutilation. It reduces the collector value of a banknote, in some cases damaging it to an extent that it is no longer collectible. Contrary to any claims otherwise, folds, creases and writing cannot be removed effectively from a banknote.

Buyer beware is the rule. Unfortunately it is generally the novice collector who ends up being stuck with overpriced cleaned notes.

So learn how to grade a banknote!

General References
and Further reading

Books on banknotes.
1. *"Guide to the Currency of Ireland Consolidated Bank Notes 1929 – 1941"*, Young D., Stagecast Pub., Dublin, 1977.
2. *"Guide to the Currency of Ireland Legal Tender Notes 1928 – 1972"*, Young D., Stagecast Pub., Dublin, 1972.
3. *"Irish Banknotes – Irish Government Paper Money from 1928"*, Mac Devitt M., 1999.
4. *"Irish Banknotes – Irish Paper Money from 1783 – 2005"*, Mac Devitt M., Third edition.
5. *"Irish Numismatics"*, various issues, published by Young D., 1968 – 1986. A hugely valuable resource for anyone interested in Irish coins and banknotes.
6. *"Paper Money of Ireland"*, Blake B. & Calloway J., 2009. Hampered somewhat by the lack of an index and inaccuracies in its treatment of Irish Legal Tender note issues, it is recommended to those who are interested in Old pre-1928 Irish Notes and Northern Ireland Notes
7. *"The Banknote Yearbook"*, various editions, published by Token Publishing.

Books on related subjects
8. *"Banking in Nineteenth Century Ireland, The Belfast Banks, 1825 – 1914*, Ollerenshaw, P., Manchester University Press, 1987.
9. *"Bicentenary Essays Bank of Ireland"*, Lyons F.S.L., Ed., Gill & Macmillan, Dublin, 1983.
10. *"Currency and Central Banking in Ireland 1922 – 1960"*, Moynihan, Dr. M., Gill & Macmillan and The Central Bank of Ireland, 1975. A very useful reference of the period.
11. *"Forgotten Revolution – Limerick Soviet 1919"*, Cahill L., O'Brien Press, Dublin, 1990. Essential reading for anyone interested in the Limerick Soviet in general.
12. *"Root and Branch Allied Irish Banks Yesterday, today, tomorrow"*, AIB, Dublin, 1979.
13. *"The Bank of Ireland"*, Hall, F.G., Dublin, 1949.
14. *"The Belfast Bank 1827 – 1970. 150 Years of Banking in Ireland"*, Simpson, N., Blackstaf Press Ltd., Belfast, 1975.
15. *"The Irish Pound 1797 – 1826"* A reprint of the Report of the Committee of 1804 of the British House of Commons on the Condition of the Irish Currency, Introduction by Whitson Fetter, F., George Allen and Unwin Ltd., 1955.
16. *"The Old Private Banks and Bankers of Munster"*, O'Kelly, E., Cork University Press, 1959.
17. *"The wolfhound Guide to the River Gods"*, Healy, Elizabeth, Wolfhound Press, Dublin and IABC, 1998, ISBN 0-86327-642-3. A book about the river masks which appear on the reverse of the A Series Legal Tender Notes and on the C Serise £10 note.

X. The Annual Reports of The Currency Commission and The Central Bank of Ireland, Irish Government Publications.
Y. The Statement of Accounts of The Currency Commission and The Central Bank of Ireland, Irish Government Publications.

Index